Author, posed as instructed. See page 102

ERNEST RAYMOND

Please You, Draw Near

Autobiography 1922-1968

CASSELL · LONDON

CASSELL & COMPANY LTD
35 Red Lion Square, London WC1
Melbourne, Sydney, Toronto
Johannesburg, Auckland

PA- 663712

RAY.

S.B.N. 304 93391 0

Printed in Great Britain by
Cox & Wyman Ltd
London, Fakenham and Reading
F.269

For
DIANA

ACKNOWLEDGEMENTS

I have to thank the Society of Authors, literary representative of the Estate of A. E. Housman, for permission to quote a stanza from his *Shropshire Lad* and another from his *Last Poems*. My thanks also to *The Lancet*, Ltd, and to their authors, Drs Christopher Hardwick and Oswald Lloyd for permission to publish parts of a scholarly description of an operation on my infant son.

E.R.

CONTENTS

ILLUSTRATIONS

Author, posed as instructed. See page 102 *Frontispiece*

I

1

APOLOGIA

The first volume of my autobiography, *The Story of My Days*, was intended to stand alone. It began with the very odd surroundings of my birth; told of my adventures in the First War and of my passion to become a writer; and found a natural close in the fine, if freakish, success of my first book. That in my plan was to end the story—and a very pleasing end too, at least for the author.

So remarkable a change in my life did the success of this first book *Tell England* effect, enabling its author to fulfil the ambition of twenty years and give his life to writing quietly in a study, that the succeeding years appeared to offer few excitements comparable with those in the original volume. This, I told myself, had held within its compass the unfolding of family secrets, the story of a hidden and irregular love before my birth, and many strange experiences granted to me by the First War in remote parts of the world, while in a second volume I should be little more than a man at a desk, and in the Second War no more than a hopelessly confused lance-corporal in London's Home Guard.

Back then to the old occupation of writing novels.

But that first autobiographical volume had such a friendly reception from those to whom I showed its typescript, including my agent and publisher, that I began to wonder if, after all, there was a place and a justification for a second volume—this one to be 'positively a last appearance'. And while I was in this uncertain mood I received a letter from my novelist son, Patrick, in terms which slowly but persistently, as I read them, tipped down one side of the balancing scales. His words were, 'When I had been with Diana the other day she said you were thinking of a second volume of autobiography. A fine idea—and I see just how it might be done—indeed I had thought of it before: not quite straight autobiography, more a literary retrospect which might (why the hell not?) repeat the success of *Through Literature to Life*—' this was a little book published way back in 1928, which was good in some parts, I still think, and sadly dubious in others, but it did enjoy a surprising and lasting success. 'I haven't a copy of that book here,' Patrick went on, 'but I remember it was sub-titled "An Enthusiasm and an Anthology"—at least I think it was. I think you could make a lovely book if you brought in all the things in Literature you have most enjoyed,

3

all the more interesting things of your literary career, and perhaps many of the ideas you have learned about writing—and hung them on a thinnish thread of autobiography. An "enthusiasm" from the perspective of—what? Not old age, certainly, but at least your eightieth year—a summing up after fifty years of experience. It would be a lovely book to write because you could bring in so much of value—and it would give you the additional pleasure of anthologizing and autobiographing. I am certain it should be seen from the fixed point of your eightieth year. Prospero laying down his staff (you can always dig it up again like an old professional). It goes thus, you will remember:

> *Alonso:*   I long to hear the story of your life,
>   which must
>   Take the ear strangely.
> *Prospero:* I'll deliver all;
>   And promise you calm seas, auspicious gales
>   And sail so expeditious that shall catch
>   Your royal fleet far off—My Ariel, chick,
>   [i.e. Ariel his art]
>   That be thy charge; then to the elements
>   Be free, and fare thou well. (*Aside*)
>   Please you, draw near.

Perhaps the last words could be the title. Why not?'

The scale went down.

Why not attempt this? A Meditation on fifty years devoted to the craft of literature, and a record of such adventures, excitements and joys as come to a settler in that curious, eccentric, disorderly but fascinating country, the Book World, with perhaps, ever and again, a consideration of what one may call, with no derogation, the 'tricks' of the writer's trade. And, of course, after thought, I began to remember that some remarkable things had happened to me, and some remarkable people been met, in the course of forty and more of the world's most terrible years. Convinced then—or trying to be—I started to write a second volume while the first, *The Story of My Days*, was still in the press; it was duly published, and its welcome seemed to justify this hope that its readers would be willing to hear a little more.

If you are one of them, and this is so, please you, draw near.

2

THROUGH LITERATURE TO LIFE

The four or five novels that succeeded *Tell England*, though not without (for me) some amusing or acceptable parts, were not, as wholes, good enough, and, were it possible, I would cheerfully see them pulped. None of them had an idea within them so strong and so moving—however immaturely handled—as that which is the central backbone of *Tell England*—the sacrifice for England's sake of a generation of schoolboys. Nor, while writing them, had I learned the thousand-and-one skills that can be deployed in the creation of a novel. I am not sure that I have yet learned them all, though to date I have published more than fifty books, because it is a truth to say that never am I plunged deep in the writing of a novel but I discern some new method, twist, or narrative 'trick' whereby the narration can be bettered, and the suspense, the hidden evocations, the tale's whole significance heightened; and I sit back and wonder that in all the years I have never perceived this particular 'skill' before. One is a learner to the end. That is why all professional novelists are impatient (though decorously silent) when someone says (as someone does every second day) 'If only I had the time I could write a marvellous novel.' Such a one does not realize that in first-class cricket, before you can bat like Jack Hobbs, you must have spent days and days and days in the practice nets, and days and days on minor fields, so as to learn every twist of the wrist, every turn of the hands, every swing of the feet, before you can steer the ball to any and every corner of the field. And what practice has been necessary before you can play a violin on a concert platform—this is something that almost sickens the imagination of us lazier men. The wrong done to a perfect batsman in his crease is that the more elegant and exquisite his strokes, the easier they look and the less credit the ill-informed give him. 'I'm sure I could do that.' So with a beautifully constructed and slyly written novel. The ignorant think they could write one in their spare time. They can write a good letter, so what more is there to learn? 'Give me a pen and some sheets of paper, *and* the time, and I'll write you a magnificent novel.'

But it is not like that.

This little discursive book, *Through Literature to Life*, though, like its fictional companions, not wholly satisfactory, must have a chapter to itself because of two remarkable consequences that sprang from its publication.

Here is the story of its origin. I had a friend who was the editor of the *Teachers' World*, and he asked me to do a series of articles on Literature that would be of help to his readers. I didn't want to do this; I wanted to devote myself to the novel in hand; but he said, 'Let us at least discuss it,' and he dined and wined me so well that, mellow in the beneficent evening, and over the cognac, I promised to do it, 'provided I could give no more than a Monday morning to each article and write it in the simplest colloquial terms'. He, mellow too, accepted this condition, and in the freshness of the morning and in the clear light of day, I was not too pleased with what I had consented to do. But there it was: I had given my word and I had to honour it; but I have always said that I wrote *Through Literature to Life* with my left hand while my right was busy with what really mattered to me, my current novel. And yet this small book, written with my left hand was indeed destined to lead me through literature to a new fullness of life.

It is the only book which I typed straight on to the typewriter, an article each Monday morning, and there an end. Away to the post with it, and let's get on with the novel. But it may be that this quick careless writing gave it a spontaneity and a readability. Methuen's saw the articles in the *Teachers' World* and offered to publish them in book form. My good publisher, Newman Flower, got wind of this and offered me a better sum. Years later he confessed to me that he didn't really want the book but 'wasn't having one of his authors in another publisher's list'. The little book was published in the autumn of '28 and, to his surprise, and certainly to mine, ran into four impressions before Christmas. It was still in print in the sixties, while the 'current novel' (thank God) had long been dead, buried, and forgotten.

The first of the two remarkable consequences was an invitation from the Executive Secretary of the National Council of Education in Canada, a Major F. J. Ney, to address a Conference on 'Education and Leisure' which was to be held in Victoria and Vancouver during ten days of April 1929, my subject to be 'Literature and Leisure'. He made clear to me that all the costs of first-class travel over the Atlantic and across the width of Canada, and all hotel expenses where hospitality would not be available, and all incidental expenses incurred by me in travelling were the responsibility of the Council. This most excellent man asked only that I should give two major addresses to the Conference, one in Victoria, one in Vancouver, and 'perhaps speak a little about the Conference at little gatherings' in Montreal, Toronto, and Winnipeg, while on my way to the West. After the Conference, he said—almost apologetically —there would be a 'rest' of some days for me at Toronto University before the long journey home.

No small invitation to appear out of the distant blue: first-class comfort all the way across the Atlantic, and from the Atlantic to the Pacific; nearly three weeks' luxury stay in the cities of Canada—did ever so tall and branching a tree spring from so small a root?

Having accepted with a surge of delight I travelled from Euston, London, to Vancouver Island in a fashion that transcended any previous imagining of mine—so far was it beyond my means then—and indeed so far has it stayed ever since: a first-class state-room on the Canadian Pacific liner, *Duchess of Richmond*, a seat of honour at the captain's table, a private room on the Can-Pac trains across Canada, and at every breathing space during the five days journey all the overwhelming hospitality for which the American continent is famous.

I went to Canada alone, my wife being unable to leave our two children then but four and six years old. There is no doubt I could have taken her with me had she been free to go, because all the delegates were the honoured guests of the Canadian Pacific Railway in ships, trains, and hotels, and many had their wives with them. It was only while travelling on the train to Winnipeg that I learned who were the other delegates coming from different parts of the world; and it was an excitement to know that the principal delegate would be Sir Rabindranath Tagore, poet, sage, and great exponent of Indian culture. (Sir Rabindranath had, in fact, disowned his knighthood in protest against the action of British troops who had fired on rioters in the Punjab, but no one in Canada took any notice of this.) Others were Sir Aubrey Vere Symonds, Permanent Secretary of the British Board of Education, Dr Rushbrook Williams representing the Indian Chamber of Princes, Comte Serge Fleury, Attaché of the French Ministry of Foreign Affairs, Sir Charles Grant Robertson, Vice-Chancellor of Birmingham University, a Mr Toyokichi Foukuma from Japan, and a Mr Bruno Rosetti representing Mussolini's Fascist Italy—so blind were we all in 1929 to the terror that was coming. The thirties had not yet broken.

As I considered the names, my heart began to shake, my breath to shorten, and I hastily repaired to the notes for my various addresses. It was the Vice-Chancellor of a university who upset my breathing most.

My first speech of any importance was in Winnipeg. On my arrival there late in the afternoon, tired with travel, I was met by the local representative of the Council and told—merely *told*, look you—that I was to be the chief speaker this same evening on 'England' at a patriotic dinner. It was a dinner organized by one of the many loyalist societies in Canada—was it 'The Daughters of Empire'? Some such name. And only two hours in which to prepare a speech worthy of them. Two hours while unpacking, bathing, and dressing. To make matters worse Prohibition reigned in Canada at this time, so that I could hope for no Dutch courage from cocktails and wines white and red. I would have to make my speech on iced water. In all my life I have never been free from some apprehension before making an after-dinner speech, but usually the initial cocktail—and perhaps a second—and the table wines and the cognac with the coffee have afforded help. But iced water! And the honour of England on my shoulders.

As I took my seat, which was on the right of the chairman—no more conspicuous place—I saw between him and me a tall microphone and —these being the early days of broadcasting when public-address systems were rare—I asked him what this portended. He told me casually, indifferently, unsympathetically, as though busy with more important thoughts, that my speech was to be broadcast over half of Canada.

That was not a happy dinner for me: excellent foods which I could hardly swallow; iced water which served only to ease a drying mouth; flattering words about 'our guest', which, for me, were rather like the last kindly words from a chaplain on a scaffold to a victim on the drop; then the microphone placed in front of me by a disgustingly unworried toastmaster; and I was on my feet surrounded by a great hush—a silence like that on the still bottom of the sea.

But the speech went well. In response to my agonized inquiries at the station the Council's representative had said, 'All you need to do is to say all you can think of in praise of England, and make some jokes about Scotland; they'll love it, and applause will greet it all. You've "told England"; now all you've got to do is to "tell Canada", ha, ha, ha.' So friendly, so charming, and so easy to say two hours before the feast began.

And yet he was exactly right: this is just what happened. I said things in my speech about England that I could never have uttered before an English audience; things which would have stirred in their thoughts such comments as, 'Oh, *wow*!' and 'Come off it.' But here in Canada each laudation of the homeland stirred bursts of applause; the applause encouraged me, and I heard myself laying on the patriotism thicker and thicker; a patriotism which is deep and genuine in me but not, as a rule, spoken in public like this. The speech received a generous American-style ovation, but I was thinking as I sat still through the long applause, 'Lord, Lord, that was altogether too fruity, too syrupy, too sweet.' And even as I was thinking this, the applause having died, my chairman drew the microphone towards him and said, 'Well now, it's my pleasure to announce that Mr Raymond's speech was broadcast over our province and beyond it by the Spearmint Chewing Gum Company.'

§

My five days journey across Canada—or was it six?—left me a lover for ever of that magnificent country: first the timber-lands of Ontario, all maple, spruce, and pine on range upon range of hills; then the prairies—in Montreal they had said to me, 'You'll be bored stiff by the prairies, there's nothing but damn-all everywhere for hours and days as far as the eye can see'—but on the contrary I could hardly take my eyes away from their beauties of changing colour and light, and their beauty of gentle rhythms like the slow, low heavings of a peaceable sea beneath all the dome of the sky. And then the total contrast as the long train climbed and climbed into the heart of the Rocky Mountains, twisting up their gorges and over their passes and along their flanks past rushing salmon rivers—and so down into the coastal region and British Columbia, so leafy and domestic, so like England with its homes and gardens, despite the neighbouring mountains, and, as everyone told me, 'more British than the British'.

The Conference opened in Victoria on Vancouver Island. As I stepped off the boat which had brought me from Vancouver I met for the first time Major Ney, the Council's Secretary and the organizing genius of this Fourth Triennial Conference: a middle-aged man in a bowler hat which, to me, seemed strangely civilian and out-of-place, after those limitless prairies stretching from sky to sky and those gigantic Rockies attempting the very face of Heaven. But within the first ten minutes I learned that under the bowler hat was a brain and a will of indefatigable energies that would drive the Conference like a galloping chariot, with a friendly and grateful but unrelenting whip for his horses, the delegates. This was Friday, 5th April, and we had hardly shaken hands before he told me quite simply and naturally and un-anxiously, like the gentleman on the station at Winnipeg, 'The big Conference Service will be on Sunday, and I've put you down for the sermon.'

'I? *Me?*' I gasped. '*Me? Why me?*' Did he then know that I had once been in Orders?

'No!' he exclaimed in a surprise like mine. 'Were you really? But this is splendid. You'll know how to do it properly. And it'll be an important service. The Governor-General, Lord Willingdon'll be there, and the Lieutenant-Governor of British Columbia with his ministers, and all the delegates of course, so you can be sure the Cathedral will be packed to its doors. In Orders, were you? I knew nothing of this. I just wanted you to give a sermon on the lines of your *Through Literature to Life* which exactly suits our topic "Education and Leisure". Really, this is a great piece of luck. In Orders. Well, now; fancy that.'

I think my only answer was a murmur, 'But gosh!' and 'My God...!' This was Friday afternoon; in the evening there was to be a Reception by the Governor-General in the Parliament Buildings; Saturday we were to be taken on a drive round the island, before an Official Luncheon given by the Government of British Columbia; the same evening would see the great Opening Session of the Conference in the Royal Victoria Theatre; Sunday morning at eleven o'clock—the Conference Service, preached at by me.

And this was a Conference on Leisure.

No one could have been more understanding than my gracious hosts in Victoria. I begged to be allowed to stay shut up in my room while I struggled to produce a sermon as I dressed for the Governor-General's dinner. I seem to remember that, in their sympathy and understanding, they sent me up milk laced with whisky. Whisky, under Prohibition, was allowed in private homes.

All the next day I grabbed at half-hours between Drive, Luncheon, afternoon hospitalities, the Opening Session, to compose and compose the sermon—but more interesting to describe than my strains on that agitated Saturday is this great Opening Session.

Every seat in the large theatre was occupied, and more people stood compressed against the walls of parterre, circles and gallery. All were come to see and hear Sir Rabindranath Tagore and their very popular Viceroy, Lord Willingdon. On the wide stage at some distance from each other Sir Rabindranath and Lord Willingdon sat on either side of

Colonel the Hon. Henry Cockshut, President of the National Council of Education. The Colonel after his introductory remarks withdrew from the stage and left its vast space to two figures only, the Governor-General and the sage from the East. Never before, I thought, had I seen so perfect a contrast between a high gentleman of the West and a high gentleman of the East: Viscount Willingdon, a slender and handsome man, in his full evening dress with orders and decorations, and Sir Rabindranath in his flowing yellow robes with his long white hair, patriarchal beard, and the serene face of a contemplative saint.

Lord Willingdon made a witty speech in which he deplored that he had devoted most of his schooldays to Leisure rather than to Education; and then it was the turn of the East to speak.

Sir Rabindranath's long address, difficult at times to follow because of its profundities, amounted to a quiet assault by an Eastern visionary on the restless hurrying of the West in pursuit of a materialist progress. It contrasted the time devoted to this purely materialist progress with that which should be given, in a world of Truth, to Man's highest spiritual destiny. Some aspects of progress were excellent: Man had found himself limited and restricted by the mere processes of natural selection, but—'he broke the prison wall open, declared his sovereignty, and refused to be content with the small pittance allotted to him by Nature, just enough to carry on a narrow programme of life. He unlocked the hidden resources and utilized them for his own indomitable purpose. This much is not materialism; it is the conquest of matter by the human spirit which refuses to acknowledge the limits to its power.'

But this spirit of progress became truly materialist and a menace to Man when he was meanly overcome by the profit it promised instead of perceiving its great spiritual meaning, which was that he had now achieved a divine right to transform the world so that it became a home for the intellectual and spiritual growth of Man. In the realm of wisdom neither dimensions, number nor speed, had much relevance because the human mind was matured only by patient self-control and concentration of faculties. 'It is only in a width of leisure that invisible messengers of life and light come bringing their silent voices of creation. A fruit in an orchard gains its inner quality of perfection, its flavour and mellowness, not by any impatient ignoring of time but by surrendering itself to the subtle caresses of a sunlit leisure.' Time might be money, as we liked to say, but wealth came from leisure. All high civilizations were living wealths that had been harvested from the deep soil of leisure. But now—

'Man seems to be building his Prosperity on the ruins of his Paradise.'

As he closed and sat down I thought that here on Vancouver Island overlooking the Pacific I had come as far west as possible, and in a great golden theatre which might stand as a gaudy picture of the ambitions of the West, I had met the wisdom of the East.

After this piercing oration by a world poet I felt that my sermon next morning to another immense audience would be a much humbler offering, though true enough, I can still believe, as far as it probed.

Like the speech in Winnipeg the sermon was well received by this hearty and generous people, but also I think, because it was a relief and easier to follow than the far greater profundities of Sir Rabindranath. It procured me the honour of an invitation to luncheon with the Willingdons in their vice-regal train in which they would travel back and forth across the continent from Quebec to Vancouver. After luncheon Lord Willingdon showed me the two charming berths for himself and his wife with a shutter in the intervening wall, at pillow-level and no bigger than a book, through which they could enjoy a last talk before sleep.

When after delivering his address Sir Rabindranath returned to India by ship from Vancouver, there was trouble at some American port— was it Seattle?—as to whether he, a coloured man, could be suffered to land. Here was racial prejudice reduced *ad absurdum*, when cruder 'whites' chose to consider as their inferior a man who was intellectually and spiritually high above most of them.

After my sermon in Victoria I was conveyed back across the strait to Vancouver so as to deliver it all again at the largest nonconformist church in that city. The friendly minister was there at the port to meet me, and he walked me back to his big church telling me all the way how many thousand dollars it had cost to build, how many thousand dollars its faithful people provided yearly for its upkeep, and how many thousand people (probably more) I should find in my congregation that evening.

His estimate was no exaggeration: the church was as packed as theatre and cathedral had been. A ladies' choir in gowns and caps sang beautifully, but what I remember most was the minister's prolonged extempore prayer. Deprived, since I was to preach, of the ever-enlarging volume of spiritual 'uplift' swelling within him, he vented as much as possible of it in this mighty prayer, which—or so it seemed to me as I wondered where to cut *my* address—lasted for some twenty minutes. It blended most admirably a minister's worship of his God with a chairman's introduction of the evening's speaker. 'We ask thee, Lord, to aid and inspire him who is to address us this night, having come many thousands of miles from the dear homeland of England where he has enjoyed so remarkable a success with his first book, *Tell England*.' Do I do him an injustice, but verily I seem to remember that, further inspired on this point, he went on to say, 'Already he has addressed our brethren on this important subject in Victoria and we thank thee now that we are to have the privilege of hearing a dear young brother speak on Literature and Life, a matter of such great significance in the spiritual lives of us all.'

3

HAZEL

At the end of the Conference Major Ney told me that Messrs Dent were going to publish a book which would contain all the addresses delivered, and he asked me to write the Foreword to it. What I wrote there will serve now, I think, to sum up this lively Seminar, and close the record.

'There is such an abundance of reading matter in this symposium that it would ill become the writer of a foreword to add unnecessarily to it; he has but to mix a small cocktail and offer it to the guests (who are at liberty to decline it) and then announce that dinner is served. But he does hope that many will sit down to the meal because he has the vividest record of the huge gatherings which partook of it in the spacious Vancouver theatre and seemed enthusiastic about their experience, and he remembers the queues of hungry hundreds who on certain afternoons and nights (for the meal lasted eleven days) were unable to find even standing room in the theatre, and turned disappointed away. In the final accounting, which took place (need I say it?) over a banquet, all who had spoken at the Conference were agreed that its most impressive feature was no single speech but the great audiences which, day after day, and night after night, crammed the theatre from parterre to roof. They were agreed upon another thing: that this was a Conference on Leisure, and there was no leisure about it. None: the man who organized it saw to that. In my memory the Conference always pictures itself as a concourse of people following the happy, if wearied, figure of Major Ney through densely wooded regions of oratory in search of the Secret of Leisure. Cheerful and not unexcited pilgrims, they followed him down into dales and up the difficult gradients (and some of the speeches were quite steep); of a truth it might be said that they toiled after him into Italy, France, Germany, India, Japan and Australia, and once or twice perhaps into Utopia; but they were an applauding and determined crowd, and I believe they were nearly all in at the death. Their guides—by which I mean the orators who had come from the Old World and the New— were refreshed by some three banquets a day, spread by all the generous-hearted societies of Canada; but the great multitude of listeners had no such resuscitation, and they came on, enthusiastic, resolute, undismayed. All of which seemed to me very right and wise: the Victoria–Vancouver Conference on Leisure in 1929 was not the first illustration in the world's history that they who would find something of value must often lose it to begin with; that they who would seek to give something to the world must be ready to deny it to themselves; and that all immortal garlands are to be run for, not without dust and heat.

Whether the secret of Leisure was found during this mighty trek I am not prepared to say; but of this I am certain, that not a man went away from the Conference, after the 'Dismiss' was sounded, whose being was not the larger for all that had been offered him; whose mind was not stirred to wonderings and doubtings about the organization of his own life, than which nothing better can happen to any man.'

§

The Conference over, I was given my week of 'rest' in Hart House, Toronto. Hart House is a residential hall attached to the University. One might call it a fine club, were not 'club' too small a word to comprise all the arts and interests that have their home in, or derive from, Hart House. (I suppose it is all the same today, but I am writing of forty years ago.)

It was in Hart House, Toronto—or rather on the doorstep of Hart House—that there issued the second remarkable—and indeed overwhelming—consequence of my little book about literature and life.

In Winnipeg, at Bishop's Court, the home of Archbishop Matheson, Primate of all Canada, I had met his young daughter, Margaret, and she had said to me, 'When you stay in Toronto I must arrange for you to meet my friend, Hazel Reid Marsh,' and, as if in eager encouragement, she added, 'She's an awfully pretty girl.'

These words had fled from my mind all through the restless Conference, but on the first morning after my arrival at Hart House, and as early as ten o'clock, a manservant came to my comfortable bedroom study and said, 'There's someone come to see you. A young lady.'

'Oh, yes?' I said, wondering who this could be. 'Where is she?'

'She's waiting at the door.'

(Is my memory playing tricks when I say that in those days the threshold of Hart House was the ultimate limit of any feminine approach?)

I went down the stairs to the open door, and there on the sacred threshold stood a girl of nineteen or twenty: tall, slender and more than 'awfully pretty'—as beautiful, I thought, as anyone I had seen in the whole width of Canada.

She apologized for this early appearance but excused it by saying that Margaret Matheson had insisted that she must come at once and see if there was anything she could do to make pleasant my days in Toronto. 'Was there?'

Was there? Was there ever a more unwarranted question? As if anything could be more inviting and delightful than to spend some days in the company of such beauty.

I spent *all* my days in Toronto with her. She brought her small car to the Hart House door and took me with much local pride to all the interesting places of her city: to Parliament Buildings and Government House and Upper Canada College, St James Cathedral and St Michael's Cathedral, and along the only road in Toronto that winds—for every other street is severely rectilinear—the road that wound along the north shore of Lake Ontario and by the harbour where the big ships lay that navigated the Great Lakes. And God bless Toronto for its green places and fine parks: for the wooded river valleys of the Don and the Humber; for the Riverdale Park by the Don with its Zoo; and for the park on the Lake Shore Road beyond harbour and sternly regular streets, because it was in these green places we would stop the car for hours, and talk together, she telling me the whole of her life from her birth in Sault Ste Marie, between Lakes Superior, Michigan, and Huron, and then saying, 'Now tell me all about yourself'—all of which sounded prosaic enough after those grand romantic Western names. There was never anything more than happy talk during these long sessions in her car, sometimes under the stars after a meal together, but let the truth be stated simply: when on my last day she drove me to the station and put me into my train to Montreal, *en route* for England, there were tears in her eyes; and I was more in love than ever in my life before.

Through literature to life indeed.

§

I must complete the story of Hazel quickly. In any case our happinesses together were forced to spend themselves within two brief years; and after we had said good-bye and lost sight of each other for ever, tragedy waited all too near.

In the next year, 1930, Major Ney, the indefatigable, brought a large body of Canadian young people to Europe that they might see something of London and Paris and go on to Oberammergau for the Passion Play. Hazel wrote to me that she was coming too, and, as she arrived independently of Major Ney's multitudinous circus, I was able to meet her at Euston, give her a luncheon, and take her to a matinée of *Bitter Sweet*, then running at His Majesty's Theatre. She had to share the hotels of Ney's wonderful rout, but she gave more of her time to me than to that excellent father and guide. Now it was my turn to take her in my car to places in England I longed to show her. A lover of Sussex, I took her to some of its quainter villages, which drew from her the usual transatlantic ravings; to Brighton as our most typical sea-side resort; and then to the summit of my loves, the long ridge of the South Downs, culminating for us in Chanctonbury Ring, where she lay in my arms under the famous beeches. Hazel was never my mistress in the usual sense of that word—I could not bring myself to seek this from her youth—but she lay often and long in my arms.

Fred Ney invited me to go with his train of girls and boys, as his Council's guest, to Innsbruck and Oberammergau, to Salzburg, Munich, and Paris. Thus, unperceived, as we hoped, Hazel and I were able to be much together in several parts of Europe, and though I have never returned to Innsbruck, Munich, or Oberammergau there are places in Paris haunted for me by her presence to this day.

After the return from Paris Fred Ney, ever irrepressible, invited me to undertake for his Council, a lecture tour across the whole of Canada that autumn. I had seen Canada in the spring; I must now see it in the glory of the Fall. One should not let the years pass without seeing the wonder of the autumn tints in Nova Scotia and New Brunswick. There would be lectures in eighteen Canadian cities, and others in the remoter universities, Mount Allison, Dalhousie, and Acadia. The whole tour would last six weeks. Finance was all that I could wish.

My first visit to Canada the year before had raised in me a love for this vivacious and dynamic young country (so American in its outer garment, so British at heart—save for those parts of Quebec which were French at heart but charming too)—it had secured my affection even before I saw Hazel standing on a doorstep in Toronto; and now I loved it more because of her. So I accepted the offer gladly and made ready to return to it in the first days of October.

When Major Ney returned to Canada with his shining comet's-tail of young people, Hazel deliberately remained behind. She would try, she said, to find some secretarial job in London. For this she had few qualifications but I suspected she had one which would win her what she sought: her beauty. In this guess I was right; she was soon given a job in a well-known office building in London which I will not name but which, like those places in Paris, remains haunted for me as I pass by. She found a home for herself in a girls' hostel in South Kensington. And so, on a day in October, we were able to invert the last year's scene on Toronto's station: then she was seeing me off to my country, England; now, on a Euston platform, she was waving me off to hers, with a smile and the same tears.

Almost daily our long letters crossed each other, on the Atlantic or somewhere on her continent, but as the time approached for my return, hers contained the sad little seeds of the end. Soon our meetings would have to stop; she could no longer endure the deceits involved nor the pain which a discovery had caused to another; she knew that it was 'not in her' to take me from a loyal wife or from my two young children now at enchanting ages, and was sure also that it was 'not in me'. When I was back in England, could we have a few more days together, so as to make easier the final parting, and then—the end?

This is what happened. We had a few happy-sad hours in London hotels, for it was winter now—and then for our last time together, we spent two full days in a suite of the Grosvenor Hotel—only apart during the night that intervened. We mealed and dined in our favourite Soho restaurant, I assuring her that I would never enter it again after these visits (and I have never been able to, in forty years). The first evening we went to the theatre where the play was Maugham's *The Breadwinner*; and we managed to laugh at some of its jokes. The last night we went to a night club, for which she put on her best evening dress, and maddeningly lovely she looked—to me. We danced together, drank champagne together, and listened to the principal cabaret artist who chanced to be the Red-Hot Momma, Sophie Tucker, singing 'Nobody's going to make a shooting gallery of me', and 'Nobody loves a fat girl, but oh, how a fat girl can love'. Here and there we laughed. Then we danced again, speaking little; or we sat together watching others; and the night wore on, both of us unwilling to say we must rise and go. Somewhere about three in the morning I took her to her hostel, and there on another doorstep, other than that threshold in Canada, it all ended: one prolonged embrace; she opening the door quietly with her key; she, Hazel, standing for a few seconds framed in the doorway and attempting a smile; the door shutting.

The last I ever saw of Hazel.

In the days after this she was stronger and more sensible than I was. I sent her gifts and letters, but she insisted that the break must be complete so that Time could work its healing and help her gradually to forget. She accepted my first gift, a gold signet ring as a memory, but other gifts she returned with my letters unopened. In a letter to a good friend of mine who was in our confidence, and to whom she was willing to write, she told him that her recoil from the pain of it all was working some loss of her love—but this my heart has never allowed me to believe.

I went off with a party of friends for winter sports in Lenzerheide, hoping to find distraction, but all the while, and for months afterwards, I was telling myself, 'This can't be the real end. A love like ours which had filled us, and was still filling me with the lover's sense of an ever-unbreakable "oneness", must have some meaning and purpose; it could not end in nothing like this; like water pouring away into a desert sand, to lose all existence and use and issue for evermore. Something which we could not foresee would happen . . . something that at present looked impossible. . . .' To my good friend I remember saying, 'It doesn't make sense. The whole thing seems like a lie in life'; and he answered more wisely, if unacceptably, 'It does make *some* sense. You have *had* something. You've both had something.'

'No,' I persisted, 'it isn't the end. It can't be.'

But it was the end, and with a finality beyond all our imaginings.

All this was in the winter of 1930–31. Eight years afterwards, in the autumn of '39 as the war broke, I received a letter from Helen Ney, Major Ney's wife, saying they were in England, and would I come to lunch with her and a friend of Hazel Marsh's—'you remember Lois, don't you?'—at their South Kensington Hotel which, strangely enough, was not a hundred yards from the doorstep in Queensberry Place, on which we had said good-bye. For most of the meal the talk was lively, natural, and commonplace, but towards the last Helen Ney dropped, as it were, casually, the words, 'By the way did you know that Hazel Marsh died two years ago?'

I sickened but covered my secret feelings with a 'No?' and a 'Surely not. She was so young.' I don't know that I have ever acted better, or that any unknowing person could have guessed that my heart within me was dead for a little too. You see, I didn't know how much, if anything, Helen and Lois had known of our hidden love; but Major Ney told me later that this luncheon had been arranged by both of them that they might break the news to me. In a voice meant to suggest that it was no more than secondary news, I asked, 'But how did it come about? Two years ago? She was still in her twenties.'

Hazel had married an Englishman some two years ago, they told me, and died giving birth to twins, who both died with her. All three lay now in one coffin, buried in Brompton Cemetery.

I maintained coversation, behind a mask of ease, and even at moments, of laughter but aching, aching, all the time to escape and get away to Brompton Cemetery.

So strange it all is: Brompton Cemetery was only about a mile from where we were sitting—a mile along the old Brompton Road, a mile from our doorstep in Queensberry Place—so that Hazel haunts the whole of South Kensington for me.

I got away and hurried to the cemetery. All the way there I was feeling sad, and even surprised that on the day that Hazel died I must have been in Damietta at the Nile's Mouth, and no sudden picture of her in my mind, no vision of her face, had appeared to me. In the cemetery office the man at the desk said, Yes, he remembered the funeral well because it was so sad: a young mother with her two newly-born babies. I went the way he directed and found the grave, and—strangest of all—it was barely a hundred yards from that of my father who in my childhood had the whole of my love.

Much of this story, disguised, found its way into my novel *Gentle Greaves* which is, I think, my favourite novel just because of this. Besides its thoughts of Hazel (though 'Gentle', the heroine, is different in character) it holds in the figure of General Allen Mourne the truest picture of my father, and thus it embraces the two deepest loves in the first half of my life.

So they lie not far apart, the two people I had loved. My father had been buried there—the story is told in my first volume—all of twenty-six years before Hazel appeared. In that quarter-century I had made unsuccessful attempts to love properly, but for the most part had sublimated all desires in the passion to write novels that would be acclaimed—and loved. Hazel was the only person who shattered the sublimation, and for her brief time occupied its place. Summing up, all I can say is that for these few months she fulfilled every dream and need of mine, even though the natural accomplishment of love was evaded by both of us; and it is indeed a strange thing that she lies so near my father. Her name can hardly be deciphered on the stone now, for it was only cut and not leaded, and the weather of thirty years has almost erased it. But I can decipher it: 'Hazel Reid Marsh. Wife of . . .'

Tout passe. Still, as my friend said, 'You have had something.' Something which has been able, during these hours when I have been writing about it, nearly forty years afterwards, to recreate for me all its exquisite sweetness.

4

ADVENTURES OF A PLAY

One day before I left for Canada I was pacing up and down the long drive of the little cottage I had built in Sussex, while I puzzled over the plan of a new novel. And somewhere between the front of the cottage and the six noble beeches that lined my garden rail, and accounted for my purchase of the site, there leapt into my mind, uninvited, an idea for a play.

I have said that the four or five novels which followed *Tell England* were less than good because they lacked a single central inspiration as worthy as that which drove the writing of *Tell England*—however inadequately it was honoured. But this sudden idea that stopped me on my garden path, and held me still, was a fine one. It had everything. It had to perfection the 'unities'—unity of place, of time, and of subject. It had the ultimate in drama, forcing its characters into the extremities of themselves, as they faced, in a sudden moment, the blackest Reality of all—death. Entitled *The Berg*, the play would put on the stage, with no break in time, the last two-and-a-half hours on the *Titanic*. From the moment when ice-blink is first observed on the horizon, through the grinding passage of the iceberg along the side of the liner, to the final minutes when those left aboard, after the last boats have gone, await the end.

My mind heating with this inspiration, I decided I would try, while losing none of the drama, to make it a play of ideas. There would be two principal characters, one a young Church of England parson, the other a genial but atheistic old philosopher confined to his wheeled-chair; and each of these, faced of a sudden with Reality at its darkest, would give his view of it, and of God, and so dramatize the deepest conflict of all.

I still think there was nothing but good in this idea; the only trouble was that the author had not skill enough to handle it perfectly. With the drama he could not go wrong, but as yet he had not grasped what manner of talk would come like gunfire across footlights, and what would resolutely refuse to cross them. The result was that the grand drama of death and human conflict faded ever and again behind a fog of talk. And then the people coughed.

Even so, the play, which in my excitement I completed in a few days, had its successes. It was accepted at once for publication in Benn's

22

Contemporary British Dramatists series; on publication it was accepted by Jack de Leon's company for a week's try-out at the Kew Theatre; Sir Godfrey Tearle consented to play the old philosopher; and after its first night at Kew it was accepted for production at His Majesty's. Its short run at His Majesty's exposed its weaknesses; but before the run was over it had been bought by British International Pictures for a film. And for years after the West End run it enjoyed a fair success on the road, in the repertory theatres, and among amateur societies.

When it turned up at the old Brixton Repertory Theatre, I took my two children to see it. And an excellent rendering the theatre's company gave it. But there was a moment of anguish for one single member only in the large audience: the author who knew every line of his play.

The old philosopher, in his wheeled-chair, was on the stage, facing the audience and talking with another character. His manservant, Pointer, was due to enter and pose an alarming question to his master, but, alas, he was 'off' and had missed his cue. I expected a shocking hiatus in the play, a silence from all, a dismay in the audience, but I did not know how real old troupers deal with an emergency like this. Noel Carey, playing the crippled philosopher, turned round and exclaimed 'Pointer! Oh, where the hell is that man? Is he ever around when wanted? But, my God, if he were here. I know what he would say—' and here he treated his companion to a splendid mimicry of his servant's cockney accent and grammar. 'He'd say, "Gawd, sir, excuse me, sir, but you told me that this boat was safe as 'ouses but one of them engineers has just said as how that's all His Eye and Betty Martin. He says it's eye-wash to keep the people quiet because the boat's got a 'ole in her bows as long as from 'ere to the middle of next week."' The other old trouper fed him with improvised lines and laughter till the missing Pointer entered, wiping his mouth—but I suspect this is an ornament added by me, after telling this story so many times—after a pint down in the green room; and Pointer proved no less equal to sewing up a tear in the play. 'I 'eard what you said then, sir. 'As she reely got a 'ole in her, or were they kinda kiddin' me?'

'Of course they were,' his master rejoined. 'People like to tell an alarmist story. Even if she has a hole she has water-tight bulkheads ...' and the play ran easily on, no one but me aware there'd been these elegant leaps over unexpected hurdles by all.

Nearly always the amateur societies wrote charming letters asking me to let them perform the play without payment as its profits were going to a charity, and I usually replied that I would be happy to do this for them if the Electric Light Company would provide the play's illumination for nothing, the owner of the hall forgo his rent, and the printers of the programmes present them as their gift. And who could say fairer than that?

Generally, however, I weakened and let them have the rights without fee, satisfied to have reminded them that, odd as it might seem, an author, like any other working man, had to earn a living: he in perhaps the most precarious market of all.

§

The film, called *Atlantic*, was made in three languages and a success all over the world, but I cannot remember meeting, from that day to this, anyone who knew it had anything to do with me.

Naturally, it had no use for a conflict of ideas between a parson and an atheist; it went out, full sail, for the external drama only, which was almost fool-proof and actor-proof. Dupont directed it, and the fine English cast assembled under him included Madeleine Carroll, Ellaline Terriss, Franklin Dyall, and Monty Banks. The set-pieces and crowd scenes remained the same in British, German and French editions; leading German and French actors playing in those scenes where individual lines were spoken. This was in the early days of talkies, and whether dubbing had yet been invented I can't remember.

The film was shot in the B.I.P. studios in Elstree and on a P. & O. liner in the Thames. In the studios was a huge tip-tilted tank of water in which some of the actors and actresses had to stand up to their knees for hours while a ridiculous scene was shot of the parson preaching courage to them as the waters of the ocean flooded the ballroom. Ellaline Terriss was in the water for hours hanging on to Franklin Dyall in his wheeled-chair; 'something I shall never forget,' she told me. 'The water was *cold*.'

I went once to the studios to watch the shooting of a final scene. This showed a young husband fainting after his young pregnant wife has been put into a boat while he had insisted on remaining with the men left on board. Some men seize the opportunity, while he is unconscious, to put him on to a last boat so that he may go to his wife. The lines in the play given to Ellaline Terriss, as she watches his departure (she having stayed behind with her crippled husband) were, 'God bless you, Laurie.

Go to your wife and children. What a joy for little Monica in the morning.'

To my dismay the film script had altered this to 'What a joy for little Monica tomorrow morning.'

I went to the producer (not Dupont, who was German) and asked why there had been this unnecessary change.

He objected, 'But what on earth's the matter with it? It means just the same as your line, doesn't it? What are you worrying about?'

I said, 'Of course it means exactly the same, but words have haunting overtones and strange harmonics.'

'Harmonics?' The word was new to him.

'Yes; strange echoes and harmonics, and you have removed them all from this line.'

'Good gracious, *how*?' he demanded, his eyes a blank stare.

'Because,' I said, 'the words "in the morning" have their overtones of "joy cometh in the morning" or "In the morning sow thy seed", while "tomorrow morning" has no overtones except those of the 9·15 to town.'

His eyes lit up as if gazing in wonder at a shining revelation. 'Good God,' he exclaimed, 'I believe you're right.'

'Of course I am,' I agreed. 'It's Dupont's business to be the expert in dramatic direction, the actors to be the experts in speaking, and the camera men in photography, but it's the author's job to be an expert in evocative words.'

'My God!' he said. And again 'My God!' as if still blinded by a great light. 'In the future we had better have the author around.'

So he said, but I don't know that this admirable idea has anywhere been followed.

§

When the French version was shewn at a small London theatre I went to see it and learned, with some delight, that the French, having no understanding of, or interest in, a C. of E. parson, had substituted for him a bedroom scene.

The French know when an audience will cough, and when it will cease to cough.

It was a scene I much enjoyed, so fresh and new it was to the author. A passenger having learned of the iceberg and the alarm comes hurrying back to his state room in time to find his wife compromised with another gentleman passenger. Oho! Magnificently he locks the cabin door, opens the porthole, tosses the key through it into the still but menacing night-sea, and hisses, 'Good. Very good. We three go down together.'

In short, *Atlantic* was a pretentious and grandiose film with many fine spectacular scenes and some intolerably silly ones.

5

'WE ARE ALL GUILTY'

We are all guilty: that is to say we all have a guiltiness operating deep down in the unconscious as well as some in the open light of day; and there is a tendency in us all to escape, where possible, from the Justice which sits enthroned in our hearts.

At least, that is how I suspect the unfortunate business stands.

As a result of this guiltiness, hidden or overt, we tend to adopt one of two contrasting attitudes; either we angrily condemn any criminal whose trial we are reading about, and rejoice in his punishment, or we feel always and inescapably a measure of sympathy for him, and our thoughts are something like 'I loathe his crime, but I wonder if he's as utterly bad as people make out. There is room, I suspect, for sympathetic understanding of him. Wouldn't lenience, perhaps, work more for him than rigorous punishment?'

Evidently I am of the latter persuasion, and I do not imagine it is any credit to me that I am among those who always feel, struggling within them, a sympathy for 'the man in the dock', but I can see that my instant dislike for all easy and happy punishers springs from this guiltiness in myself and from memories, awake or buried, of the too facile and impercipient punishments received in childhood. It may be, if the modern psychologists are right, that, however old and 'respectable' I am now, I am still little more than the small boy, writ large, who, after my Aunt Emily's slapping hand, stinging cane, and loud abrasive voice (as told in my first volume) used to think with passionate tears, behind his locked and disgraceful door, 'I am not as bad as they make out. I'm *not* nasty—at least not as nasty as they're saying. It isn't fair, and I hate them.'

All this, plainly, is the seed of a book that through all my first years of authorship I had longed to write; it would have as fine an integral, vertebral idea as *Tell England* or *The Berg*: the story of a man who committed just about the worst crime known to the Law—premeditated murder by poisoning—and who yet . . . It would follow him, both ruthlessly and with some ruth, from the first dawning of the murder-thought, through the murder itself, his flight, the long manhunt, the capture, the trial and conviction, and so at last into the condemned cell and the execution shed.

A title came quickly, *We, the Accused*, and I've never known whether the 'we' refers to the two prisoners in the dock, or suggests that our

Society in general, with its gravely unequal class structure, its profiteerings and exploitations, and some of its established Law, Justice, and Penology, might well, for a little, sit in a dock too.

I started the book many times but put it aside because the obstacles repelled me so. What did I know of police procedure, of criminal law, of the laws of evidence (that shocking field of man-traps, gins, snares and unexploded bombs for the amateur) or of prisons, those dark walled places so jealously guarded from all meddlesome cranks, and from such frivolous persons as novel writers by the Prison Commissioners (we are coming to these gentlemen in a minute). Lazy, I recoiled from the drudgery of research; shy, I shrank from thrusting my inquiries upon people who would rebuff me. In 1932, however, I got the early and easy domestic chapters written, but directly I came up against Police, Law, Prisons, and all the steep hills that would have to be climbed if the book was to be as authentically accurate as I desired it, I ran away again; I ran into the lanes and fields of Sussex and wrote a book which flowed easily from my pen. 1933 appeared and my forty-fourth year, with its prospect of a tiring middle-age, to say nothing of the ever possible chance of an early demise, so I started to climb again. I got a little way up the steep slopes and ran, for the third time; this time into scenes of my childhood, writing a book which came easily because I had accumulated the facts for it between my sixth and sixteenth years.

And then, in 1933, came the Furnace man-hunt. Many people will have forgotten that story now, but Samuel Furnace was guilty of a terrible murder and I did not question that he must be apprehended and segregated. Nevertheless there were aspects in that man-hunt which, for me, were nauseating in their indecency; and all my combustible stuff was well and truly fired this time; I was alight with energy for the steeper hills.

I studied Criminal Law. I read a pile of books on Police Law and Administration. Also every book written by a retired Scotland Yard detective—no small task because, one and all, they write their memoirs while the going is good. I studied these latter, not only to learn their methods but, even more, to read between the lines into the make-up of these kindly, competent, but unself-critical minds. Not one in twenty of these ex-detective-inspectors saw anything amiss in the Law or wanting in their methods. All was fine in their Scotland Yard garden. That Law and Morality, and even Law and Justice, could at times be different things—this was not a flower that bloomed anywhere in the Yard.

Next the prisons. But as nearly all the books on prisons were written by 'safe' people who were allowed facilities by the Prison Commissioners, not mere novelists (you begin to perceive a resentment) they were not of much help—one book always excepted, the weighty encyclopedia assembled by Stephen Hobhouse and Fenner Brockway, *English Prisons Today*.

Satisfied that my mind, for the present, was sufficiently stocked, I left the books for the flesh and blood of the actors themselves. I courted many policemen, and, without exception, very kind, helpful, and humorous they were. Whatever I might have felt about their powers of abstract thought, there was no questioning their friendliness, goodwill, and basic humanity. When I told them that I might be moved to guy some of their methods, they said, 'Good. Well, now we'll read the book. We hadn't intended to, really.' And enthusiastically they collaborated in its writing. One of them was kind enough to arrest me in his private parlour and, when I resisted, threw me to the ground by means of a villainous steel 'cuff' shaped like an 8. I rose, thanked him, and with a half-broken wrist, jotted down notes. Another took my fingerprints. Another cautioned me.

But most helpful and most able of all was a P.C. Simpson, an athletic young constable at Bow Street. Twenty-four years old, he guided my steps like a father. At his suggestion I wrote to Scotland Yard for permission to go all over Bow Street Police Station, and in no great while I received a courteous reply granting my request and stating that P.C. Simpson was commissioned to give me all necessary help. So P.C. Simpson took me into every hole and corner of that famous building—into men's cells, women's cells, matron's room, detention room, charge room, prisoners' waiting-room and any other place that was to figure in my story.

I still possess sheaves of closely written foolscap in which he answered in massive detail my long questionnaires. As I write now I turn over a letter in which he sketched for me an elaborate diagram like a genealogical tree, explaining police hierarchies, detective methods and delegated activities, not only in his Metropolitan area, but in all parts of the country.

It is pleasant and strange to see that this letter is written from a 'Constables' Section House' and signed in the friendliest way, 'Joe Simpson'. But today I wonder how I dared take up the time of a busy young policeman like this, and how I am daring to write of him here as

'Joe Simpson'. Because he is now Sir Joseph Simpson, K.B.E. and O.B.E., Commissioner of the Metropolitan Police.

Still, here is his letter in front of me, signed 'Joe Simpson'. So I suppose it's all right.

§

I have left this paragraph above just as I first wrote it, because it expressed my feeling then for Joe Simpson. Alas, only a few days after writing it I read that Sir Joseph Simpson had collapsed and died at the early age of fifty-eight. His whole Force mourned him. And so did I, gratefully remembering him.

§

Thanks largely to him, I felt that, as regards the police in my story, I could not now go wrong. And if I did, despite all his help, he had promised to arrest me and caution me in time.

Now for the Prisons. Or, as we might say with a different intonation, now for the Prison Commissioners. Much encouraged by the courtesies of Scotland Yard, I wrote to the office of the Prison Commission, submitting that I desired to write a serious and accurate piece of fiction, no 'thriller', and asking if they would match the help of Scotland Yard by allowing me to see a condemned cell, an execution chamber, and other places that I desired to see with my own eyes in the interest of perfect accuracy. And if they would detail some obliging officer to answer the questions I might want to put to him. Promptly I received this reply:

> Prison Commission
> Home Office, Whitehall, sw1.
> 30th April, 1934

'Sir,

With reference to your letter of the 16th instant, I am desired by the Prison Commissioners to say that they know of no objection to your utilizing any published information for literary purposes but they regret that they are unable to afford the facilities for which you ask.

> I am, Sir,
> Your obedient servant
> ....
> Secretary.'

So there it was. The tradition of the Police Service in England is to be as friendly, helpful, and open as that of the Prison Service is to be despotic and secretive. Or so things were thirty years ago.

At first I was extremely indignant. I told myself that these gentlemen seemed to have forgotten that English Justice was open and public and subject to criticism; that it was *my* justice as well as theirs; that its quality of openness and publicity did not cease the moment a man was convicted; that a serious novelist was a legitimate mouthpiece of public criticism—in short, that they took too much upon them, these sons of Levi.

Today I see their position with more tolerance. I see that they desired to protect their prisoners from any cheap exploitation and that it might have been invidious to grant facilities to one writer, however serious he thought himself, and deny them to others. I was told later that one of them phrased it, 'We don't exist to provide exciting material for novelists.' But that their rejection of me need not have been quite so prompt and peremptory was proved to me years afterwards when a charming Governor of Pentonville Prison, under instruction from new Commissioners, showed me everything that I desired to see behind his gloomy portals and answered every question I wanted to ask, for the purposes of another (and far inferior) novel I was then writing.

This rejection at the time of writing *We, the Accused* seemed a mortal blow to the book, because the final chapters would be the climax of all and I wanted for them nothing less than the factual accuracy I believed I had won for the earlier parts. Was I going to be defeated after all? Would the story never be written despite the year-by-year labours I had already given it? Plainly I would have to abandon it rather than paint a vivid and accurate picture for three-quarters of a book which would then disperse itself into a fog of guess-work at the close. This thought of abandonment was like a sickness, but what hope was there? The rebuff was complete. The prison gates were locked.

Night after night I would lie awake and tossing in my bed, as I wondered if there was any way I could outwit the Prison Commissioners and come at my information. At one time I considered seriously the commission of some offence that would get me thrust into prison where I would keep my ears open, my eyes wide, and my tongue going strong. To offer my services as a prison visitor would involve me in lies, as I knew well, because long before I had ever dreamed of *We, the Accused*, and with no ulterior desire to get 'copy', but simply because of my feeling for prisoners I had volunteered for this work, only to be met with the demand, when I stated my profession, that I would never in any circumstances make any use of what I saw in prisons in anything I might write—a condition quite unacceptable. But if I went to prison on a magistrate's order no man living could command my secrecy.

The idea was fascinating. But the problem was to find an offence which would not leave a stigma behind and so damage the book in another way. Something political seemed to be the best line, but the Act which I adjudged one of the finest in the Statute Book, the Probation of Offenders Act, might be the very one to get in my way. Just supposing that after a calculated and deliberate misdemeanour I was only put on probation to be of good behaviour for a couple of years.

So the days and nights of despair went on. There was no solution anywhere. The book could not be written. The work on it was wasted. All the heavily detailed pages provided by the charming young P.C. Simpson were useless. Perhaps some other story could one day be dug out of them, but not the story which had now possessed me for years— the story that must march relentlessly to its only possible—if terrible— close. Not only did I feel incapacitated from finishing this story, but sometimes, in my disappointment, I felt almost inhibited from writing any more novels at all.

Then came a night when through all the hours of darkness—or so it seemed—I lay tossing on my bed, racked by this belief that the book was finally and beyond hope, slain. A miscarriage. Dead before birth—and not long before birth. I awoke heart-sick because with the morning light I had fallen asleep on the acceptance of defeat.

I came down sadly to breakfast; I opened my paper; I read the front-page political news; I turned to other pages; I read about a Herr Hitler's successes in Germany and terrible tales of unemployment in the North— and suddenly, that very same morning, I found myself reading about a young man who, after being condemned to death and spending some weeks in the condemned cell awaiting execution, had just had his sentence quashed on some legal quibble. He had left the Appeal court a free man.

With a hope as huge as it was sudden I knew that if I could find this man, and that if by good luck he should prove intelligent and willing— ready also to earn a little money since he would be certainly out of work —I should have all the information I wanted, and better information than if I had got it in any other way. If ever a news-story in a paper had seemed like a miracle, it was this. I had said no prayers; I had only suffered; but this was like an answer to prayer.

How to find him? I had his name and his photograph and a mention of the crowded London district in which he had lived. No more; but I set off that morning. His name, though not common, was not uncommon, and directories showed it in several streets of that district. All right: one could ring at every house which held the name. I do not do this sort of thing easily, being always too apprehensive of a harsh and ugly dismissal, but an author will sometimes do anything, suffer anything, risk anything, pay any price, for a book which has become a favourite child of his imagination. He can even, as I have shown, be ready to go to prison in search of 'copy' for it—but only so long as his precious name isn't besmirched in the eyes of men, his readers.

I came at length to the house where he had lived when arrested, but he no longer lived there. The woman of the house told me that she thought he had gone to a neighbouring road, but wasn't sure of this, and, anyhow, wouldn't know the number of his home. On then to that road, a depressingly long one, and a knock or ring at door after door. Soon I came to a door where a woman, opening to me, said with an instant and wide-eyed interest, obviously wondering if I was The Police: 'Oh yes: the young chap who was sentenced to death; yes, he's—' she hesitated for a moment—'he's at No. —; jest along there.'

With a trembling heart I went to this new door, pressed its bell and stood on its threshold, wretchedly nervous of being addressed by some insolent ruffian as an interfering busybody and told to 'make off with myself'. What was I going to find? Steps were approaching the door; it opened; and before me was the face I had seen in the papers. An attractive face, looking much younger than it had seemed in the Press photographs; a face of good boyish features and bright intelligent eyes, but . . . the pallor of it! One had heard of 'prison pallor'; was this the pallor of the condemned cell? At first the intelligent eyes were startled into unhappiness; I am tall and in my civilian clothes may well have looked like a C.I.D. detective. So I quickly, though with stuttering and embarrassment, told him what I was seeking and suggested he sent me away at once if he wanted to be done with all that had happened to him in the last few months . . . but if he would like to earn a little money . . .

I had hardly said this before he told me that he was out of work and would be only too glad to be earning something as he was married and had a wife to keep. He invited me into the 'parlour'—as far as I remember this was his mother's house—and I went with him into a spotless, polished, proudly kept little room, where in a glass-fronted bureau and on the mantel were cups and medals he had won as a Boy Scout. I knew as I sat myself in a comfortable chair, and he on a hard chair opposite me, that Good Fortune had welcomed me into this home and was seated here with us. Here, plainly, was a working-class lad of exceptional brightness and understanding. He promised to tell me everything I could possibly need about the last days of a condemned man, and he showed me a framed picture of his pretty young wife which 'had been with him in the C.C. [condemned cell] all the time'. On it was written, 'I am with you always'.

We sat and talked happily together in this neat and polished room. I told him that the character in my book, an elderly man and already described in more than five hundred pages of manuscript, could have no resemblance to him. All I wanted was the furnishings of his life in the Remand Prison, the Old Bailey cells, and, above all, in the condemned cell—together with all the functioning of the prison service around him. We did not touch on the question of his guilt or his innocence before at the last moment the Appeal Court discharged him; his conviction had been quashed on some legal point only, but it was not for me to trouble him further by probing into his alleged crime. And even if he had admitted guilt to me and agreed that his escape was lucky I should have had some sympathy with him. The charge against him amounted to what I believe is called 'constructive murder', and it made nonsense to me.

First remember that this was 1934, in the aftermath of the Great Depression, when the unemployed were still numbered in millions; when you could see them standing about in the streets, often with despair and revolt in the eyes of the older men and a sourness and aggressiveness in the eyes of the young who after a year or two in a boy's blind-alley job had come up against a high dead wall with a legend 'Not Wanted Any More'. This young man had been successful at school, highly praised in the Scout movement, and well thought of in his few working years—but now, in his early twenties, he was cast out, not wanted, dispossessed of his right to use his talents anywhere; one of a whole generation of disinherited young. Some of the young men thus 'left to rot' had after a year or two of loafing on the dole, put an end to it all by suicide; others rebelled against a Society which dealt with them like this, and turned, in a mood of bitter self-justification, to crime.

Within these circumstances the charge against this boy, married and in need of money, was that he and another lad had been induced by an old and experienced criminal to help him in the burgling of an old woman's house where money was supposed to be hidden. Neither of the boys was accused of being a violent type; neither had any previous conviction; and neither knew—or in their defence they denied that they knew—that the old lag was going to gag the old lady. She died under the gag, and all three were charged with her murder. 'Homicide by an act of violence done in the course of or furtherance of a felony involving violence, e.g. robbery with violence, is murder'; so says the Law—or so it said then. I believe that this long-held, and even proudly held, doctrine that an act done in the commission of a felony which causes death is in all cases, and for all associated with it, murder is now frowned upon; and that the verdict on these young men would be 'manslaughter' today: for all I now remember, and, indeed, for all that I was capable of understanding then, this was what caused the quashing of the boys' conviction. There is much in our Law to salute as well as much to query; more on the whole, perhaps, to salute.

This able young man and I worked in friendliness and understanding for weeks afterwards. I asked nothing of his emotions at the trial or in the condemned cell. These were my business, and the murder in my novel was quite unlike that with which he was charged. What he gave me in letter after letter, responding to my long questionnaires, was the whole curriculum of his days, throughout his weary wait in Brixton Remand Prison, throughout his trial at the Old Bailey, and throughout his last weeks in the condemned cell. He drew for me scale plans of the hospital ward at Brixton, the exercise yard, the visiting rooms, the Old Bailey cells, the prison van, the C.C. at —, and the condemned man's screened pew in the chapel of the same prison. (He had actually taken his 'last communion' there.) He sketched in the furniture of the cells even to the position of the electric light switches on the walls. He gave me his meals in detail and told me all the games he had played with his two attendant warders in the C.C.

In fact he helped me as efficiently, intelligently, and exhaustively as did P.C. Simpson, but in, so to say, the opposite field.

Not once in our co-operation did he show any vindictiveness towards the prison officers; rather he stressed that they all, from the Governor downwards, strove to make his last days on earth as touched with kindness as might be.

For more perfect safety I brought all his information to the test of a retired prison governor's comments, that I might have the outlook of the jailer as well as the jailed. It was to this most kind and helpful officer that I am indebted for the minutely exact details of the last hours of all, from the arrival and 'imprisonment' of the executioner himself to his grim testing of the executing machinery, and his terrible work in the morning.

§

Often I find myself saying that to write one page of a novel easily and convincingly one must know enough to write five hundred. Then that which distils on to the page is a quintessence.

I now felt I had knowledge enough to allow imagination to run free. I was ready to complete the book. On this principle, 'knowing enough to write five hundred pages in order to write one', I had set the 'pre-criminal' chapters in a social milieu and in landscapes that I knew with the completeness of child or lover. My later boyhood was spent in an environment of struggling middle-class gentility, and some five years of my youth were given to schoolmastering. All my childhood had been in a London suburb; all my manhood I had loved the downs and weald of Sussex, the outcrop of greensand hills that fronts the North Downs of Surrey, and the rough mountains and lakes of Cumberland and Westmorland. My murderer therefore was a little struggling school-master in a suburb of London but his heart was with the wealden villages and the Sussex hills he had known as a boy; and when the murder was done and terror came to live with him, it was to these places that he fled; when the hunt was up and the bloodhounds hard behind him, it was over the South Downs that they chased him; when the hunt pressed close it was to the woody slopes of the greensand hills that he went to earth; when the police surrounded the greensand hills it was to the empty mountains of Cumberland that he slipped away; and when they came upon him at last, it was on a lonely fellside near Buttermere Hause.

Therefore he is not Crippen. Those who must hang a label round a novel announce that *We, the Accused* is based on the story of Crippen's murder of Belle Elmore and his flight with Ethel Le Neve. It is not. Crippen was an American-born dentist, and I know little about America and nothing about dentistry, save from its receiving end, and that the pain there can be damnable. Crippen fled straight from London to Antwerp where he took ship for Canada. My book could never have been so magnificent a story as that of Crippen and Le Neve. That flight across the Atlantic with Ethel dressed as a boy, that wireless message out of the Atlantic, that chase of the two fugitives by Inspector Dew in a faster ship while the whole world watched, that pilot boat approaching the *Montrose* off Father Point with Inspector Dew disguised among the men in a pilot's jacket while Crippen watched innocently from his deck rails, that meeting of Inspector Dew and Crippen on the deck just as Canada and safety were in sight: 'I think you know me, Dr Crippen' —these things are too good for fiction.

Why? Because it is only by their having happened in real life that they can be believed, and the first necessity of serious fiction is that it should be believed. That is why no novelist can excuse an unlikely episode or a too violent coincidence in his novel by saying, 'But it is based on fact; it actually happened to someone I know'; because in real life the fact that it happened is the solvent of disbelief, but in a novel no such solvent is present. And once your reader says, 'How impossible!' your hold on him is lost, and all your fine descriptions, all the best of your dialogue, all your skilful character-delineations are lost with it. The thread is snapped and your pearls are scattered.

The book completed, the copy delivered, the proofs corrected, I went off to Spain, not guiltless, for the first time in my writing life, of a flight from the day of its publication. It had meant so much. It had cost so much. Not one of the seventeen books preceding it had meant so much or cost so much. The hope of a wide recognition for it had a hard task to fight down the dread of a wide rejection of it. Or, worse, a dull neglect of it. A still-birth or its early death would have been like a death of half myself. That day of publication I spent in a little sunny cove near Palma in Majorca. And that evening I went on board ship to return through the night to Barcelona. We arrived at Barcelona in the morning, a beautiful Friday morning in May. After breakfast on board I went ashore and wandered along the ramblas, those boulevards of Catalonia's capital. They were as crowded and noisy as ever; and the sun glinted down on the newspaper kiosks under the trees. Among the colourful newspapers and magazines that made a frame for a black-eyed houri in one of these booths (Carmen's young sister, surely) I saw the *Continental Daily Mail*. Was it likely, was it possible that—no, of course not—not here in Barcelona. . . . Of what interest to any of the Americans, British, or

Spanish in Barcelona was an outpouring of mine—one of thirty or more novels published that week? The book, just now, might be the whole of my life; it was scarcely so much as a grain of sand to anyone here. Still, a writer always hopes for the impossible, dreams the impossible, and, even though telling myself that I expected nothing, I gave the houri the price of her *Continental Daily Mail*.

The first page that I opened at a suitable, an innocent, distance away had a headline splashed across it covering a most generous review by Compton Mackenzie. I count that moment, under Barcelona's sun, and amid the din of a Spanish rambla, one of the most gratifying I have known.

And Compton Mackenzie was the first swallow of a pleasant summer for *We, the Accused*. There were some grey days in that summer, of course. But the reception of the book did not disappoint me. It had the widest and most favourable criticism of any book I have published. It was even awarded by the Book Guild their gold medal for 1935; the last that admirable institution awarded before it went out of business. It has since been translated into many languages, and was later—a most pleasing Summer of St Luke—the choice of the *Sunday Times* readers, at the invitation of the newspaper, for its list of 'the Hundred Best Crime Stories'. But perhaps what gave me as much pleasure as anything else was the closing sentence of a review in the *Manchester Guardian*. It said, 'Given another half-dozen novels as powerful as this, and in fairly quick succession, and the death penalty should be a thing of the past.'

Two very happy outcomes of the book's publication may be—or let me be honest, *must* be—slipped in here.

The first was that soon after its publication I became friendly with Sir Alexander Paterson, the Director of Convict Prisons, and later the great reforming prison commissioner, and he told me that the Commission had read the book and, remembering their refusal of my request for help, had wondered how on earth I had achieved for the final scenes that same 'photographic accuracy' which I had needed for all. As far as I remember, I did not, in my still somewhat unreasonable exasperation with the Prison Commissioners, give the true answer even to the liberal and tolerant Alec Paterson, but offered him only an annoyingly gratified smile. I preferred that his colleagues should be left in some doubting wonder as to the ways in which their paymasters, the People, could outwit their secrecies.

The other happy thing was that one of the greatest of all defending counsel, Norman, later Lord, Birkett, read the book and said that it was the only 'criminal' novel he had read without finding in it one legal or technical error. As a matter of fact a distinguished magistrate, Claud Mullins, did find a mistake in the Magistrate's Court scene, but it was not a large fault, and one blemish in 630 pages may perhaps be forgiven.

6

THE YOUNG P.E.N. AND A CONSEQUENCE

As I look back on the years of writing and publishing that book there comes another thought which has no kinship with these happy memories of some praise and some achievement. It is a dark thought, and it is charged with a surprise that seems more akin to self-contempt or at least to a guilty dismay.

Throughout those years of dreaming, writing, publishing and savouring a fair success, say from 1930 to 1936, I had little thought for anything but the book. It filled my mind like a mountain and there was scant room for the world outside. To be thinking only of one's dreams and ambitions, and untroubled by all that was to be! To be glancing hardly at all at the world outside and the monstrous things that were creeping towards us. To be in Barcelona in 1935 and unaware. Unaware that the war for Europe, for the West, for the World, would open on this same soil the next year. In '33 Adolf Hitler had become Chancellor of Germany and in '35 at least his shadow lay across Europe. In '34 the Fascist Heimwehr had overthrown the Socialist Government of Vienna after three days of civil war. In '35 the first of the Italian black-shirts embarked for East Africa. During '35 and '36, while I remained preoccupied with the sales of *We, the Accused*, Germany passed the Nuremberg Laws against the Jews; Falangist rebels, fighting the legal Spanish Republican Government, were spreading from town to town in the south of Spain, from Seville to Cadiz and Malaga, and over Spanish Morocco to Melita and Ceuta and the Canary Islands; Italy declared her war on Abyssinia and marched from victory to victory; and Haile Selassie, Emperor of Abyssinia, uttered his great cry, 'If my tardy allies never come, then I say prophetically, and without bitterness, the West will perish.'

But, looking back, I see that I was far from alone in concentrating on my own ambitions and watching these dark events with interest certainly, but only a secondary and peripheral interest. One sees something all too like my preoccupation with private dreams and ambitions in Sir John Simon's betrayal of Manchuria to the Japanese, the recoil of the nations from pushing sanctions against Italy to the utmost, and Mr Eden's advocacy of 'Non-Intervention in Spain,' accompanied by a jest about 'the War of the Spanish Obsession'. Non-intervention in Manchuria, reluctant intervention in Abyssinia; non-intervention in

Spain. 'Let's all mind our own business and poke no noses into other people's actions,' we seemed to be saying. 'We are not required to be the conscience of the world. Where is our moral responsibility for what is happening in Germany or Italy or Spain? The Jews in Germany are Germany's own problem, and let the Spaniards decide for themselves what sort of Government they like best. Hitler and Musso may be helping the Spanish rebels but Stalin is supporting the legitimists, so it seems to balance out pretty well. Let 'em all get on with it among themselves.'

But the mindless, monstrous tide was coming in. And in the end the tardy Allies had to rise if the West was not to perish.

§

The activities of an institution called 'the Young P.E.N.', of which I was to become the President during these years before the tide flowed in, have their bearing on this strange, unheeding, or only half-heeding, insular apathy that shrugged and teetered on our side of a comforting English Channel.

I had been a member of the International P.E.N. Club almost since its inception in 1922. The P.E.N. Club ('poets, essayists, editors, novelists') was founded by Mrs C. A. Dawson Scott, a formidable but large-hearted lady who had written several novels, but none of them can compete as creative achievements with her creation of this world-wide association of writers vowed to the total freedom of expression by writers all the world over.

All of us who remember Catherine Dawson Scott's resistless but amiable onrush through a room (or through life) know that she gave her whole heart and strength to causes that seemed right to her; but probably only those who sometimes sat and talked with her in quiet knew how big her heart was, and how much of her driving force drew from a quick maternal tenderness and a strong maternal impatience. Unless I used to read her wrong she belonged to a fine type whose inconsistencies seem necessary for the advancement of mankind. Essentially autocratic, she loved freedom and democracy and worked for them autocratically; loving toleration, she would fight for it with an impatience that touched intolerance; and, knowing that peace was the only habit for sane people, she enjoyed the battle for it. She instanced splendidly the truth that, despite all its sorrows, life and liveliness are one. A fine strenuous life, Catherine Dawson Scott's, and one of which her children, whether born of her body or her spirit, whether in her home or in the International P.E.N., can be proud.

She ensured the P.E.N.'s early success by persuading—or perhaps 'amiably bullying' would be the phrase—John Galsworthy, then at the height of his international fame, to become its President. Thereafter it advanced in strength till it had its branches in more than forty countries. In 1928 its devoted secretary, the playwright, Hermon Ould, conceived the idea of a junior branch for literary aspirants who had yet to make a name and qualify for the parent organization. First he got Galsworthy to write to the London papers announcing the formation of this new society. Galsworthy never failed to do anything demanded of him by Mrs Dawson Scott, or asked of him by Hermon Ould—indeed I find it difficult to imagine anyone disobeying Mrs Dawson Scott or disappointing Herman Ould. Galsworthy wrote:

'Sir, As President of the P.E.N. Club I have pleasure in stating that there has come into being a society called "the Young P.E.N.", affiliated to the London P.E.N. Club. It will consist of young writers and literary aspirants, never more than twenty-nine years old, not as yet eligible for the P.E.N. Club itself, and many of whom will not so far have had any work published. It will exist to foster creative talent, bring young writers together, and give them a chance to meet with young literary folk of other countries—for I do not doubt that the example of this idea will be followed in many of the countries where the forty-two centres of the P.E.N. Club exist.'

There had been comic discussion among the members of the old P.E.N. as to what their junior branch should be called. One suggestion was 'the Nibs'; another that the Mother Society should now become 'the Fountain P.E.N.'.

Since, according to my estimate, one in every three persons is a literary aspirant, there was quite a crowd at the gate of the Young P.E.N.—so much so that at last the qualification for membership demanded that a candidate must have had some creative work, however small, accepted and published somewhere.

The Young P.E.N.'s first president was E. M. Forster, the second Lady Rhondda, and the third Bertrand Russell. These were big names and inevitably figure-heads rather than active participants. The club's

Hon. Secretary who, like all such, carried the whole weight of the organization on his back was Erik Warman—he was 'Erik' then, but the 'k', a temporary aberration, has fallen like a spring blossom, and he is now, as christened, Eric. For the purposes of this chapter Eric unloaded on me all the filed documents covering the years of the Club's existence, and I was proud to read among them a letter from Hermon Ould to Erik in which he writes, on the occasion of E. M. Forster's withdrawal, 'Whom will you get now? I am not at all sure that it wouldn't be a good idea to have somebody young who would take an active interest in the Young P.E.N. because he really takes it seriously. What about Ernest Raymond?'

But as yet Erik was after a bigger name than mine, and Forster was followed by Lady Rhondda, she by Bertrand Russell. It was not till 1933, on the resignation of Bertrand Russell, that the Club asked me to be its President. My filed letter accepting the invitation has perhaps some interest since it expresses an attitude to modern literature which is, for me, the same now as it was thirty-six years ago. 'My dear Erik, I am much honoured by the invitation of the Young P.E.N., and will certainly try to be as well-behaved a President as possible. My real fear was that I was not really—or at least to younger writers would not appear to be—advanced enough. Naturally I think I am with the future rather than with the past, because I think the future will swing back a bit towards old values and old canons of art; but in the eyes of the young to believe this is surely grossly old-fashioned. But at least I *understand* their extremist opinions....' A postcard I found among the files also interests me now because it shows the prices obtaining then in quite good London restaurants: 'Somewhere in the train between Purley and Three Bridges it occurred to me that my announcement to the company last night that I had to leave to catch a midnight train followed with unbecoming haste upon my announcement that the waiters were about to collect the money. A bad beginning for a President. Please, what do I owe?' The answer requested four shillings for the dinner and seven-and-six for my bottle of wine. I remained President of the Young P.E.N. till, like many another bright young hope, it died in the War. And very happy I was among all these eager, merry, irreverent young people. Among our early members who made big reputations later were Pamela Frankau, Rodney Ackland, Margery Sharp, Diana Young, Godfrey Winn, Selwyn Jepson, Allen Lane, and Giles Playfair. Among the famous who came as our Guests of Honour to address us at our dinners were J. B. Priestley, Elizabeth Bowen, John Brophy, Harold Laski, Alex Comfort, Miles Malleson, Flora Robson, Ernst Toller.

But these gay young people, with Erik for their bell-wether, did not only feed in restaurants: in November 1929 I see they were dancing in the Century Ballroom in Regent Street at a cost of five shillings each, or nine shillings for two, inclusive of refreshments; and again in 1931 on board the *Friendship* that once plied between London and the West Indies, but now lay moored in the Thames against Charing Cross Pier. Later we are dancing at the Arts Theatre Club till one o'clock in the morning.

I have all the copies of the *P.E.N. News* published during this last ominous and uneasy decade between the wars, 1930 to 1939, and easily the most entertaining contributions in almost all these issues is that dealing with the Young P.E.N. and coming from the merry, witty, impudent pen of Erik. For example:

'Our dinner was marked by a very happy speech from Mr Galsworthy who was our Guest. I have watched many celebrated writers addressing the Young P.E.N. and I have come to the conclusion that they look upon the affair as a far greater ordeal than facing their own people in the Fountain P.E.N. or indeed any other collection of writers in existence. This must be due to our youth and only goes to show that the most condescending of them are, at heart, secretly troubled by what the younger generation is thinking about them. Our reply to this feeling is to try to "combine a pose imperious with a demeanour nobly bland". In other words we rise to the occasion and allow our Guest (strange how that word arouses prickings of the conscience) to believe that his worst fears will be realized.

'The point of all this is that at this dinner things did not go according to schedule. Mr Galsworthy did not appear in the least awe-stricken at the sight of so many young critical faces. Nor was his speech at all deferential or apologetic. On the contrary, while not uttering a word to which anyone could take exception, he deftly succeeded in creating an atmosphere which more or less told us to go to the devil. This was all very unusual, but the strangest part is that we loved it. So does man weary of adulation, and so will the great men always hold their own.'

Or this:

44

'At our last meeting Mr Horace Shipp talked to us about the "Form of the Novel". Or, rather, to use his own expression, he "thought aloud" on the subject. He was quite frank as to his motives which were, apparently, to lead us on to giving him advice which would be of value in his own work. This was quite refreshing, especially as most of our visitors cloak the fact that they wish to pick our brains by pretending to teach us something. As I have mentioned before in this column, there is no end to the attraction which the youthful point of view has for the established authors. It must be the constant dread that they are becoming senile, at least in their ideas. Ah well, we can afford to be generous. They cannot last much longer.

'But Mr Shipp was quite open about it, and thus we became quite a happy family intent upon helping him out of his difficulties. The result was that, of course, we did learn a great deal and were happy to discover that even so illustrious a person as a prominent dramatic critic comes across the same stumbling blocks as we nonentities.'

And finally:

'Three reckless members of the Young P.E.N., Allan Taylor, Alex Henderson, and W. E. Warman are producing a new monthly review. It will cost a shilling and will be called *David*, as it is hoped that it will be a permanent menace to the Philistine.'

But, alas, in this case it was Goliath, the Philistine, who killed David after only a few sharp stones from his sling. The Philistine defied the armies of the living God, giving poor David's flesh—and it was a pretty flesh too, lovingly printed and produced—to the birds of the air and the beasts of the field.

Erik could be serious when an occasion cried for it. Perhaps our most memorable occasion was a dinner in October 1933, when our Guests of Honour were Ernst Toller and Harold Laski. There is a significance in that date, October 1933, which lay all too far from the sight of many of us, or was all too dimly descried by the rest of us, but not by our two guests, both of whom were Jews well known to half the world. Nine months before this date Hitler had become Chancellor of Germany; eight months before it the Reichstag burned; in September, all over Germany, the vile persecution of the Jews began to rage like a fire or a plague; and even as we sat down to dinner that day the Assembly of the

League of Nations was passing, or had passed, a resolution of aid for all 'Jewish or other refugees from Germany'.

Ernst Toller was one of those refugees. A short man of square powerful build, he wore his hair picturesquely long—but not so long as that which turns our heads and sets us gaping—or gasping—in the coiffures of our young men today. The hair framed a large, handsome, intelligent face. I always thought that in an assembly of writers Ernst Toller *looked* the part better than most—who, in general, didn't look it at all. Though he had fought enthusiastically in the 1914 war, he had been driven by the horrors he had witnessed, and by the deepest emotion in him, a compassion for humanity, to become a pacifist and a leader in the Red Rising of 1919 in Munich, for which he was sentenced to five years imprisonment in a fortress. In prison and out of it he wrote the best of his revolutionary plays—revolutionary in manner as well as in matter. I have seen only one of them, *Masses and Men*, but recognized it as a fine example of the new Expressionist Drama, alight with the Toller compassion. I had met Toller at congresses in Budapest, and in Dubrovnik this same year, 1933, and learned at both of them that he was among the great orators of the world.

At Dubrovnik the American delegate, having in mind the Jewish persecutions in Germany, the burning of books, and the apparent submission of the German P.E.N. to the Nazis, proposed a resolution which concluded with the words: 'We call upon the International Congress to take definite steps to prevent the individual centres of the P.E.N., founded for the purpose of fostering goodwill and understanding between races and nations, from being used as weapons of propaganda in the defence of persecution inflicted in the name of chauvinism, racial prejudice, or political ill-will.'

The German delegates said they would support this motion on condition that there was no discussion; but H. G. Wells, presiding, was hardly one to have this subtle dust thrown into his eyes, and he ruled, 'Whosoever wants to discuss this resolution shall be free to do it.' Toller rose, amid great applause, and suggested, subtly too, that the resolution should be passed unargued, and he would only speak afterwards. Let the resolution go on record as passed. The Germans, at sight of this famous Jew, this leader in the Munich rising, this orator who could sway a multitude, announced, 'If Herr Toller is allowed to speak at all we must withdraw our support of the resolution.'

Wells, just about the least likely person in Europe to bow before bullying or blackmail, repeated quietly and calmly, 'Anyone wishing to speak will be permitted to do so', a statement which evoked a storm of applause in the course of which the German delegation walked out of the hall. Then Toller spoke, and it was the finest speech of the whole stormy occasion.

Subsequently I travelled with him from Dubrovnik, *via* Cetinje and Cattaro, and over the mountains of Hercegovina to Belgrade; and it is particularly sad to read Eric's story of our Young P.E.N. dinner in that October of '33 because of what followed almost immediately after it.

'The largest gathering the Young P.E.N. has yet achieved was on the occasion of the opening dinner of the season. We met in order to welcome two famous men, Herr Ernst Toller and Professor H. J. Laski. Mr Ernest Raymond in his introductory remarks referred to Herr Toller's triumphal tour through Montenegro and Southern Serbia after the last P.E.N. Congress, and went on to announce that Herren Ernst Toller, Leon Feuchtwanger and Heinrich Mann had been elected Honorary Members of the London Young P.E.N. as an indication of our sympathy and friendship with them in their exile.

'Herr Toller then spoke and emphasized the value he attached to this expression of our solidarity with oppressed writers of another country. In a magnificent speech, full of power and feeling, he indicted the persecution of culture and called upon the young writers of the world to fight for freedom and not be silent. "It is the task of the true artist to correct his Age when it betrays the spirit."

'His audience were deeply moved by his sincerity and depth of feeling, and showed this by the ovation they gave him at the end of his speech.

'An equally brilliant discourse, though of a different kind, came from Professor Laski. He reminded us that this man whom we took pleasure in honouring might have to leave England in a few days because the Home Office would not extend his permit to remain. "What are you prepared to do about this?" he asked, and suggested we could help by letting our Members of Parliament know that there were many who strongly desired that this country should offer sanctuary to men like Ernst Toller.'

But this was not to be. Ernst Toller had to leave Britain and emigrated to New York, where he wrote an autobiography with the appealing title, *I Was a German*. Then, after the Ides of March in 1939, when Hitler's armies invaded and occupied the rump of Czechoslovakia to which they had no possible legitimate claim since the inhabitants were not brother Germans but Slavs; and when a new world war became certain, and Toller's despair for the Germany he had loved overcame him, he chose to die by his own hand.

§

In the year '34 Mrs Dawson Scott died, a dozen years after her founding of the P.E.N., and several of us wrote our tributes to her in the *P.E.N. News*. The finest of these, as can well be imagined, came from Rebecca West. 'I loved, and still love, Mrs Dawson Scott. I liked so much the way when she was old in years you could see that she must have been the prettiest young girl, plump and dimpled and smiling and fresh. She had to the end the air of that young girl as she might have been the day before she was going to the village fair; full of brisk plans, full of the tenderest hopes of lovely things that were going to happen. I never knew anybody—and this is the thing that above all makes me love her—who was so little daunted by the failure of the village fair to come up to expectations. At the end of her life, with abundant experience of its harshness, and of the stupidity and cruelty of human beings, it had still never occurred to her to doubt that there was an explanation, by the light of which all this unkind chaos would show as merciful order, and that she would stumble on this explanation one day. . . .'

1934. Sometimes one is tempted to feel glad that she did not live to see the full flood-tide of human cruelty that was about to engulf the world. Not that she would have lost heart or been deterred in her various battles: she was too bonny a fighter ever to tire or falter or lay her visions aside.

§

Just as the Educational Conference in Canada produced a strange consequence and an unexpected gift for me in the love of Hazel so, years afterwards, the Young P.E.N. played a similar part. In 1935 and '36 we were having our club dinners either in a basement below the level of the pavement or in an upper room under the tiles: in other words, in the charming basement dining-room of the Book Wine Restaurant in

Great Russell Street or in the fine top-room restaurant of the Arts Theatre Club. It was in the delectable basement room that one evening a new young writer, nineteen years of age, who had already written her first novel, was presented to me, the evening's chairman, and her first words were 'How long did it take you to write *We, the Accused*?'

'Three years off and on,' I said, concealing my pleasure, which every author knows, when he is asked to say something about one of his books. 'More, perhaps, because I twice put it aside to write an easier book.'

She then spoke of the book in enthusiastic terms which, unfortunately, it would be indelicate for me to repeat, so I will record only that I was thinking, 'This is not only a damned pretty girl, but also a damned intelligent one.'

She is now my wife. Five years later, when the war broke, we brought our lives together, and since then she has been my support and strength, and often my inspirer, almost beyond the dreams of optimism, in every field, emotional, intellectual, spiritual. I am also proud to say that she no longer writes her novels under her maiden name, Diana Young, but under mine, Diana Raymond.

7

ST FRANCIS AND THE SHADOW

1937, the storm near now, and yet I was still only glancing over my shoulder, and with a shrug, at the clouds to windward; still preoccupied with self-centred dreams of writing a book this year, next year, or some year, that would be acclaimed, remembered, and endure. In the autumn of this year the publishers of H. V. Morton's very successful *In the Steps of the Master* and *In the Steps of St Paul* suggested that I should attempt a similar 'In the Steps' book – a book, that is to say, which would be at once history, travelogue, and interpretation. I said I would willingly do this if my book could follow the steps of my favourite saint, and probably the world's favourite saint, Francis of Assisi.

They agreed, and I planned an itinerary through all the towns of Umbria, Tuscany, and the Marches; through Rieti and Rome to Brindisi; and thence to Alexandria, Damietta, and the Holy Land—all the places which had known the presence of Francis. I set off quickly so as to be in Assisi by October 4th, the *Festa di San Francesco.*

Since this safari in search of the heart and meaning of St Francis has been told in a book of 360 pages, it cannot be retold here. What interests me about it now, thirty years after its writing, is that this was 1937 and the autumn before Hitler's seizure of Austria and the surrender by Britain, France and Italy to him at Munich – the surrender of our Honour to Naked Evil. All that I have described so far, my adventures in Canada with its issue in the love of Hazel, my writing of *We, the Accused*, my happy presidency of the Young P.E.N., and now this mention of my wandering about the world in the footsteps of Francis – all of it seems to have taken place during a bright autumn evening before the dusk and the darkness fell.

Though awake, like the rest of the world, to the dreadful shadow of Nazism and Fascism now lying over Europe, I had no idea how soon it would lengthen and reach Britain, and I don't remember once thinking that my pursuit of Francis could be a journey in search of the answer to this evil. For Francis, a layman, as it were, like ourselves, unconfused by the 'two Natures in One Person' of his master, Christ, could, in some ways, be capable of a more effective appeal to a sceptical and doubting world.

Of course we were all aware of the dark cloud sinking low upon the world, we saw that the First Act of 'Something to Come' was raging in

Spain, but we in Britain were still trying to believe that we were protected from it by a ditch; the Channel dimmed our eyes and dulled our thought. Or, worse, it enabled the cynical immoralists to say, 'Best leave Herr Hitler alone. Better he than Bolshevism. Let him do our work for us, and at least contain the Communists, even if he cannot destroy them.'

As for me, wandering after Francesco di Pietro Bernadone, the Poverello, the Little Poor Man of Assisi, wandering behind a far distant voice which had said, 'Lord, make me an instrument of your peace. Where there is hatred, let me sow love,' I found comfort in the thought that art must be aloof from all merely transient political conflicts, all temporary wars and disasters, and deal only with eternal human emotions that knew no passing date. In his *Enemies of Promise* at this very time Cyril Connolly had written, 'It is a mistake to exceed the artist's role and become a political investigator.' And again: 'A lyric poet ... is entrusted with the experience of the ages; he is not a political conscript nor can he be accused of escapism if he confines himself to celebrating the changing seasons, memories of childhood, love, or beauty ... history goes to prove that lyrical poetry is the medium that more than any other defies time. Didactic poetry becomes unreadable ... but ten minutes extra thought on the choice of a word or the position of a stress may make in the lyric the difference of a thousand years.' These excellent arguments, which in normal circumstances I find unanswerable, helped to build for me a raft on which to float while others drowned.

It took Munich and the rape of Czechoslovakia and the certainty that Hitler was about to seize Poland, and above all, the butchering of the Jews, before I perceived that the Terror sweeping Europe was something more than a ruthless self-defence of Finance Capitalism against Communism; something more than the equally ruthless and unmoral methods of Communism in its retort to the Capitalist uprising; it had become an upsurge and release of something primitive, savage and fiendish in Europeans hitherto tolerably civilized; men turning against their own people as well as against their enemies, Germans torturing and murdering Germans, Spaniards doing the like with Spaniards, Italians with Italians, Russians with Russians; it was no longer a reasoned phenomenon; it had left reason behind that it might enjoy an orgy of mindless fanaticisms, supping daily of sadistic torment and murder; it was an epidemic of madness.

But in 1937 I was still a little blind to this, and in Italian towns where

Francis had lit again a gospel of love; in Damietta, at the Nile's mouth where during the Fifth Crusade he, this most famous of Christ's Fools, had dared to walk straight into the lines of the Saracens—though the Sultan had promised a golden ducat to any of his men who would bring him the head of a Christian—and preach peace and love to a Sultan enchanted; in the Holy Land where his sons still guard the sacred places, I was happy making notes for my book and leaving Europe to look after itself.

In 1937 the Holy Land was still 'Palestine', a territory mandated to Britain by the League of Nations. It stretched from the Jordan Valley to the Sinai desert and the Mediterranean littoral, and its population was roughly 900,000 Arabs and 400,000 Jews building their new 'National Home'. The present Arab kingdom of Jordan was but 'Transjordan' across the river and the Allenby Bridge. In 'Palestine' Arabs and Jews lived as rioting enemies together and neither race showed much love for, or gratitude to, their British masters—the Arabs naturally none; the Jews little. So 1937 became the vigil of a Commission set up by the British Government and the League of Nations to find some method of partitioning the country. Two years later the Partition was established. It gave most of the old Samaria to Transjordan which thus spread over the river and became the new Arab kingdom of Jordan, with the Old Sacred City of Jerusalem in its hands; for Jerusalem is a sacred city to the Moslems as well as to the Jews and the Christians. To the Jews it gave the coastal plain, Galilee, and much of New Jerusalem. Two new kingdoms, Arabic Jordan and Jewish Israel now lay side by side.

§

I was to visit the Holy Land thirty years later in the spring of 1966, and it's like a compulsion in me now to mention that on the day before we went out of Jordan and through the Mandelbaum Gate into Israel I was reading the leading article in an 'English' Arabic journal, the *Jerusalem Star*, which made me realize better than ever before the iron-hard barrier, barbed and electrically charged, that ran between the Arabs and the Israelis. It said:

'Today is the anniversary of the end of the British Mandate. This day, eighteen years ago, should have seen the establishment of the Arab State of Palestine.

'As the world knows, this desired event did not take place.

'Much has and can be written about the deceitful policies of the British Governments, entering repeatedly into conflicting agreements and always yielding to pressures at home to abrogate solemn promises to us which they knew in all justice they must keep.

'Much has and can be written about the evil schemes of the Zionists— conceived long before Europe's holocaust gave any excuse of humanitarian need—to rob us of our heritage, drive us from our homes, and expel us from the land of our fathers.

'Much has and can be written about the efforts of the Americans to aid the imperial aims of the British while abetting the nationalist facism of the Jews.

'Much could also be written about our own shortsightedness, about our persistence in feuding long after dire peril has made unity an immediate necessity rather than a distant dream.

'But today is not a day for mourning, rather for preparation. Recrimination will never lead us back to our homeland, but only determination, sacrifice and planning.

'Today must be for us a day of challenge. . . .'

Next day we went through the Mandelbaum Gate, Jordan behind us, Israel beneath our feet, and it was like crossing from a primitive Biblical century into the midst of the twentieth—into a new city built by one of the most gifted nations on earth. Remembering that article, I made a bet with my son, 'If, as the article suggested, all the Arab armies surrounding Israel attempt an irredentist war against it, the Israelis will wipe them up in a week.'

I was wrong. Two months later they did it in six days.

§

Back to 1937. That winter and in the spring of the next year I was writing the book all too comfortably behind my two ditches, the one our English Channel, twenty good miles wide, and the other my own little furrow, much shallower now but still there protecting me—the comfortable statement that my business, whether as novelist or historian, was with the things that belonged to all time rather than with those that occupied a passing hour.

8

THE PASSING OF A NATION

'Munich? Munich? What is this "Munich"?' More than thirty years lie between us and that hysterical Munich week; and who under forty today knows in full what the name of Munich recalls to those of us who were in their thirties, forties and fifties then? Young people often ask, 'Munich? Munich? What is this "Munich"? One's always hearing the word and I don't know what it's about.' To me the question is apt to recall the song of Patience in the opera, 'I cannot tell what this love may be That cometh to all but not to me'; only for the word 'love' many of us, rightly or wrongly—the argument never ends—substitute 'hate'.

Let me then tell the young something of the story in simple terms.

Czechoslovakia is a beautiful country in Central Europe, comprising some of the finest soil on the continent and abundant natural resources for its many industries. More than this, after the First World War, under its liberators, Thomas Masaryk and Eduard Beneš, its President and its Premier, it was the finest example of a liberal democratic state in Europe, a republic with president, senate, and chamber of deputies elected by universal suffrage. And Masaryk, its president, in his love of truth and wisdom and his devoted education of his people, approached the ideal of Plato's 'philosopher-king', though blessedly declining the totalitarian autocracy with which Plato would have invested him. Some of us used to say that the two best things, if not the only two good things, that issued out of the 1914–18 slaughter were the League of Nations and Masaryk's Czechoslovakia.

But . . . its weakness lay in an overspill of three million Germans, or one-fifth of its population, spread about the Sudeten mountains which, like a barrier, separated Czechoslovakia from Saxony and Prussian Silesia. And after Hitler's rape of Austria in March 1937 it was plain to all that he would next attempt the seizure of Sudetenland where lived 'his tormented German brethren'. But the high Sudeten mountains were a natural strategic frontier for the new country of Czechoslovakia; if she lost them to Germany she would be like a mouse beneath the paw of a cat.

In the summer of 1938 there was a Congress of the P.E.N. Club in Prague, and I made a point of attending it, pretty certain that I should be looking my last on Masaryk's lovable creation. Masaryk had died the previous year and at his wish, and the wish of all his people, Beneš had succeeded him as President.

To come at Prague and Czechoslovakia we had to pass through Nuremberg. We looked out from our train windows at a Nuremberg washed by the sunlight of a June day in 1938. Everywhere along its grey streets, from the windows of high gables, from the dormers in the sagging roofs, from the sills of the out-jutting storeys, hung swastika flags, their red, white and black looking insolently new against the old dusky grey. Small flags, large flags, and long falling banners; but why they hung there, and what it was all about, no one in the train could say, since it wanted two months and more before the congress of the Nazi Party would crowd the streets, the beer-halls and the arenas of Nuremberg. Incongruous they seemed, those red-and-white flags with the tormented black cross in their hearts; disconnected with the past; insulated from all previous history; sudden and modern and harsh against the old grey walls.

And everywhere in the old streets beneath them walked young Germans, in brown shirts or black uniforms or light civilian suits, but almost all of them, as it seemed to me, self-consciously stiff in posture and tread, unsmiling, and absurdly humourless with their quick Nazi salutes to one another. The sight of them hurt, somehow; it bruised one's sense of fitness; an impression difficult to formulate in words, but beneath those multiplied flags they appeared to me as something not only revolutionary, cocky, and overbearing, but also as something essentially impermanent and unstable.

When our train entered upon the Böhmer Wald, the mountain bastion of Bohemia, Czechoslovakia's chief province; and when it stood at a frontier station among these wooded hills lifting ten thousand conifer points to the sky, it was strange to wonder how soon this bastion would fall to the sallow little dictator in his mountain home at Berchtesgaden. This barrier guarded a pocket of Slavs in the rich centre of Europe; an 'inferior race' (in the eyes of the little man and of his Nazi Herrenvolk) who dared to occupy 'a fortress built by God in the very heart of the continent'. So Bismarck had called it, adding, 'Whoever is master of Bohemia is master of Europe.'

The train went through the forests and foothills and, shedding them behind, entered the clean green basin of Bohemia—an open vale watered by a glistening river. A doomed country? Perhaps, but nowhere in the vale was there sign or hint of doom. Working in the fields, walking on the white roads, were the short, stocky, flaxen Czechs. Athletic young men disported themselves in the river; trios and duos of laughing girls strolled arm-in-arm along the paths and waved to our train as it went by; and I waved vigorously back, wishing they could know I was English and on their side in all things.

Our train rolled into Prague. On the platform a group of Czech writers stood waiting to welcome us. Waiting behind them, taller than most, was a young-looking man in a grey lounge suit. Clean-shaven with rather thick lips, a nondescript nose and boyish cheeks he might have been any age from thirty to fifty. In fact he was thirty-eight. His head was bare, his hands were in his pockets, and his lips played with the stump of a cheroot. So modest seemed his place among the rank and file that, as I struggled out of the train, I supposed him to be some un-successful writer who was flattered to be a member of the International P.E.N. To my surprise, however, I was called up to be presented to him as to a leader. 'Come and meet Capek.'

So this was Karel Capek, Czechoslovakia's most famous writer; the man who had given a new word to the languages of the West, 'robot' from his play about the man-made mechanical men, 'Rossom's Universal Robots' (*R.U.R.*). Familiar as I was by now with the disappointingly commonplace appearance of most world-famous writers, I still found myself wondering that Karel Capek should look no different from any other rather putty-faced young man.

M. Capek led us towards the station doors and the street—not because he considered himself a leader, but because he was taller than the rest, and his stride longer. Courteously he helped us into two-horse fiacres and directed them to our various hotels.

Later in the garden of the Hradčany Palace I was presented to President Beneš, a small man in a pale semitropical suit and looking, because he lacked height, even less distinguished than Capek. We exchanged a few conventional courtesies not worth reporting here, but all the time we spoke together I was thinking: the tenth child of a struggling peasant farmer, he has a peasant's face; nose irregular, small grey moustache roughly clipped, the mouth thin-lipped and obstinate; a commonplace face from the fields except for the high brow and the bright intelligence in the eyes. A village schoolmaster, one might have guessed.

And yet this little man had created, not a book, not a symphony, not a city even, but a nation. Working like a mole in Paris and London, while the Great Powers were fighting each other, he had conceived, drawn up, and gradually brought into being the modern Czecho-slovakia, all ready for its liberator, Masaryk. At the Peace Conference he had expounded his creation and defended it against the statesmen of the world. With cold grave obstinacy, unruffled and precise, and, in the last audit, by sheer intellectual force, he had won his way with them. They had accepted his creation. And thereon, during twenty years, he had watched over it, without show, without noise, and without charm, like a peasant doing day-by-day the task of the day. To the side of his country he had drawn two other countries, Jugoslavia and Rumania, so that now he was the real master of his 'Little Entente' and led these nations on his rope, as a peasant leads a team of horses to the field.

And now the menace of a Second World War, and the sour glance of the German Fuehrer had made him for the moment, the second figure in the world's eye. History had selected him for its own. Adolf Hitler on his height at Berchtesgaden, Eduard Beneš in this Hradčany garden stared at each other across the Bohemian mountains. And of the two, this man was the symbol of civilization. The symbol of everything threatened with destruction.

Which would win? And what then? If he resisted the destruction and defied the threatening Hitler, it could be that we should have to march behind him, or beside him, to war. Were not France and Russia treaty-bound to go to the aid of Czechoslovakia if attacked, and was not Britain equally bound to fight at the side of France should she be at war again with Germany?

As I came away from talking with him I heard a father talking to his son. They were two of our party standing near. The young son, staring with fascination at a country's ruler, said softly to his father, 'He doesn't look much to write home about, does he?'

'No,' the father agreed.

'But he was hot stuff at football,' the boy reminded him comfortingly.

'Yes, that's true. Till he broke a leg.'

'He was almost an International at one time.'

'Well,' said the father, 'he's certainly an International now.'

§

This was June in 1938; let us move on to that autumn, to the last days of September which became the darkly troubled and then the mad Munich week.

On September 22nd our Prime Minister, Neville Chamberlain, flew to Germany to meet Hitler at Godesberg on the Rhine. A few days before this, at midnight, a decision had been reached by the Powers, without reference to Czechoslovakia, that there should be a realignment of the Czech frontiers giving Hitler the Sudeten mountains and almost all else that he demanded, but promising a guarantee of the new frontier. The Czechs rejected this decision with a furious '*No!*' No one questioned, not Beneš himself, that special consideration should be given to the Germans in the Sudetenland, but they had never been citizens of Germany, and Hitler's demand for their immediate 'return' was therefore but smoke in the eyes of the world. 'No!' said the Czechs. 'We will talk but we will not yield an inch of our land.' But the next morning, at 1.0 a.m., helpless, they accepted. Helplessly and in terror. The Czech Minister in Paris said, 'My country has been condemned without a hearing. It is a death-sentence on our independence. Our only safe frontiers will be lost, and the Germans will be thirty-five miles from Prague.' And on the next day we learned that the Prague Cabinet had been forced by their people's anger to reverse this decision to accept. They would not cede this territory. They dared not.

And so we come to the 22nd again. At Godesberg Hitler tells Chamberlain, 'My patience is exhausted. If the Czechs do not yield, I shall march in immediately. My troops will occupy the Sudetenland on 1st October and no later. And what is more, not a single thing in the Sudetenland, not a building, a factory, a home, or even one of the cattle, is to be destroyed or removed before we come.'

But the Czechs maintain their refusal and mobilize. Chamberlain flies home with little but despair in his bag. He will not accept these new exactions. Britain mobilizes her Fleet. France reconsiders her decision to default on her agreement with Czechoslovakia and announces that she will abide by it. And in Germany, on September 26th, the Fuehrer, kindled to frenzy by the refusal of the world to take its orders from him, speaks for an hour in the Berlin Sports Palace, declaring as before, as hitherto, as always, 'My patience is exhausted. Beneš has his choice between war and peace. He will surrender his territory on October 1st, or we march in. We are a different people from that which marched backwards in 1918. I told Chamberlain that this man Beneš shall no longer maltreat three and a half million Germans. Two men stand against each other: Beneš and I. *Benes und ich!* Let this Beneš accept my terms or we go and liberate our Germans. I shall be the first soldier right in front of you; and behind me, let the world know it, the German people marches in step. Stand to attention! Ready! Man for Man! Woman for Woman!'

What these two last phrases meant, or if they made sense at all, probably no one, least of all the orator, had time to consider. A prolonged study of them in the quiet of this day, thirty years later, has not succeeded in squeezing any meaning out of them. But no doubt they sounded very fine in the Sports Palace of Berlin.

That same evening I received a letter from Karel Capek and forty other Czech writers. It was a circular letter addressed to the writers of Britain.

FROM THE CZECHOSLOVAK AUTHORS
ASSOCIATION

To the Conscience of the World

'In this fateful moment when a decision between war and peace is being reached we address this solemn appeal to all those who form the conscience of the world.

'Taking our stand today upon the last bastion of democracy in Central Europe we proclaim, in full awareness of our responsibility towards historic truth, that our nation is guiltless in respect of the catastrophe looming before us. We therefore appeal to you whose function it is, above all else, to watch over what hitherto were the most cherished possessions of Europe: freedom of the spirit, love of truth, and purity of conscience. We ask you to judge for yourselves where the genuine willingness for peace and justice is to be found, and where the aggressive spirit of despotism which utilizes every device of violence and lies. We call upon you to make it clear to the public opinion of your countries that if a grievous contest is forced upon us, a small and peaceful nation, we shall wage that contest, not only for our own sakes, but for the sake of you and of the moral and spiritual heritage common to all free and peace-loving nations throughout the world. Let nobody forget that after us the same fate will await other nations and countries. We appeal to all authors, and all others who create culture, to make this manifesto known by every possible channel to the nations of the world.'

Reading this, I decided that Czechoslovakia was now, not just the name of a small country, but another name for freedom, for the right to live and speak and write as we liked.

But—September 28th. And the famous, the historic—or the hysterical—scene in the Commons. I met a friend in the street and he cried, 'It's all over. There's to be no war for anybody. It's all a wash-out.'

A sad and shaming fact to which I must confess is this: my first reaction to his words was—for all my love of Czechoslovakia—one of disappointment. I realized then that my dominant feeling in these weeks of menace had been one of excitement like a boy's at the prospect of terrific drama and thrilling days. And now the drama was to be denied to us, after all. It was as if the manager had come before the curtain and said, 'No performance tonight.' I was shocked that I could wish death for millions so that I could be excited and entertained. Ashamed, I asked him for more information, and his answer ran something like this:

'There ain't going to be no war, no war. It was the Navy that did it. We mobilized the Navy this morning, and in the afternoon Hitler decided to change his tune. There was the most amazing scene in the House this afternoon—haven't you seen the papers?—nothing like it in umpteen years. M.P.s dancing and yelling like a lot of kids promised a holiday. The P.M. had been speaking for an hour and making it clear that the fat was well in the fire when someone handed a paper to Lord Halifax up in the gallery, and he read it and immediately disappeared. A minute later someone handed the paper to the Chancellor of the Exchequer, and he poked Chamberlain in the ribs and gave it to him. The P.M. just read it and went on with his speech. He told the House that he'd sent a last appeal to Hitler and Mussolini and then calmly announced, lifting up the paper, that Hitler had invited him to come to Munich and discuss the matter further with him and Musso and the French Premier. Every man-jack in the House went mad, jumping to their feet and yelling and waving their order papers. Even patting each other on the back. It couldn't have been a greater furore if it had been a cricket match. If old Chamberlain had hit the winning boundary just when the game seemed lost.'

Chamberlain flew to Munich, as did Mussolini and the French Premier, Daladier. And in the beautiful city of Munich where the Nazi movement had first arisen the four leaders of the Great Powers, Britain, France, Italy and Germany agreed to the apprehension and enchaining of Czechoslovakia by Germany. Great sections of Czechoslovakia in its north, south, and west were to be ceded to Germany, including the towns of Asch, Eger, Carlsbad, and Marienbad. The poor rump of Czechoslovakia was to be left naked and indefensible; a succulent morsel on a plate for Hitler's next meal. Together they signed this 'pact for the orderly taking over of the Sudetenland by Germany'. That it was to be orderly, and not sudden or rude, was all they got from Hitler.

They had persuaded him to take ten days over it.

The Czechs were not even invited to join in the discussion over the pact; nor were allowed to stand in the room and watch the signatures being applied to the order for their martyrdom.

In the morning of September 30th we knew that it was all over. The final news had come at 2.30 a.m. After reading my paper at the breakfast table I walked out of my Sussex home and chanced to meet the Honorary Secretary of the Conservative Party. He knew me for a Liberal who'd had many a lively fight with his party at election times. None the less his first words to me were, 'Well, I have never thought I should be ashamed to be an Englishman.' It was a generous concession to much that I had maintained on platforms in our neighbourhood.

That evening a dense crowd pressed against the front of 10 Downing Street, cheering and singing and shouting. They had sung 'Rule Britannia' and 'Land of Hope and Glory' and 'O God, our Help in Ages Past', and when at last Chamberlain arrived in his car and waved a hand to them as he entered the house they sang, 'He's a Jolly Good Fellow' and then shouted imperiously, consistently, rhythmically, 'We . . . want . . . Chamberlain. We . . . want . . . Chamberlain.'

In response a first-floor window came alive with a promising light. All eyes swung up to that rectangle of light. Voices roared at it, yet more loudly, 'We . . . want . . . Chamberlain.'

The window went up and the Prime Minister stood in the midst of the light. Now the loudest cheering of all beat against the old house and continued, the people not understanding at first that the Prime Minister's outstretched hand was an appeal for silence. Then, as if all understood in the same instant, the cheers subsided abruptly and silence possessed the narrow creek that is Downing Street. And in his clear voice, strong as a young man's, the Prime Minister spoke.

'My very good friends, this is the second time in our history that there has come back from Germany to Downing Street "Peace with Honour". I believe—'

But he had to wait till the cheers acknowledging this, acclaiming it, had sunk again.

'I believe it is peace in our time.'

He smiled—and his was an attractive smile—he waved once more to the boisterous crowd, and retired from the window. The window shut, the light went out, and that was all. We drifted away.

Peace there might be; and peace for a few months, if not 'for our time' but 'Peace with Honour' there was not. There was no honour in throwing Czechoslovakia out of our sleigh to a howling German wolf-pack, that we could get safely away.

'I believe it is peace in our time.' With these words there seems to fade away the argument often propounded since those days that the 'Peace with Honour' achieved at Munich was really a confidence-trick whereby we gained time to amass enough armour for the fight tomorrow. If this was really what Chamberlain intended, and I find this difficult to believe because I have always accepted his sincerity, then his 'Peace in our time' was a lie to the people. And, anyhow, it was a peace won by a betrayal.

Harold Nicolson, speaking next day in Manchester, spoke for most of us. 'We have not achieved peace for a generation, we have achieved it only for six months. The mobilization of the British fleet at the eleventh hour had threatened to break the Berlin–Rome axis. We held all the cards in our hands, but we have betrayed a valiant little country and a great democratic idea.'

'Peace with Honour.' It is said that Chamberlain regretted having spoken those words, 'Peace in our time', and I can believe this, and be glad of it. In my view Chamberlain has always seemed a good old man, strangely blind. Blind to the fact that this betrayal of Czechoslovakia was a retreat from the future. Blind to the fact that at Munich the vanguard of mankind, led by him, had turned round in its tracks and faced towards the past. Blind to the fact that there at Munich three of the most civilized countries of Europe, Britain, France, and Italy, had betrayed not only a small sister country of high civilization, but the advancing spirit of Man. Munich, Munich, the name, for so many of us, is a touchstone for ever, wherewith to test whether a man believes more in Man's safety, comfort, and life than in his honour.

That dark month of September died and October broke upon a world at peace.

But a few days later a letter dropped on the mat of my Sussex home. It came from the broken heart of Czechoslovakia. Dated Prague,

30th September, and signed by Karel Capek and his brother authors, it said:

TO THE CONSCIENCE OF THE WORLD

'On this day when by the decision of four statesmen our country has been abandoned and delivered to injustice with its hands bound, we remember your declarations of friendship, in the sincerity of which we believe. Even in the difficulties of our present position we remain, and shall remain, in the forefront of Humanity's common struggle for truth and justice. We stand by our President, and without despair we fix our eyes on the tasks of the future and still remain faithful to the moral and spiritual ideas of our nation. Sacrificed, but not conquered, we charge you, who for the present have escaped our lot, to persevere in the common struggle of mankind.'

§

I have been writing this in the last days of August 1968. In that spring of '38 I foresaw a terrible impairment and mutilation by Hitler of Masaryk's Czechoslovakia, this country which had been a bright focus of liberalism, democracy, and high quiet culture, shining like a beacon in the very heart of Europe for twenty years. Twenty years, till in '38 Chamberlain spoke of it, deprecating war 'about a far-away country of which we know little.' 'Know little'! When every liberal mind in the West delighted in its existence. All its neighbouring countries had succumbed to totalitarianism—Communist, Fascist, or Nazi—Jugoslavia, Rumania, Italy, Poland, Germany... but not the Czechoslovakia of Masaryk and Beneš.

I foresaw Hitler; but not the ignominy of Munich; nor Hitler's tanks and armour ravishing the whole country on the Ides of March, 1939. Least of all did I foresee the 21st of August, this year, and but yesterday, when Russia's tanks and armour celebrated the fiftieth year, the golden jubilee, of Masaryk's republic with an exactly similar rape, enforcing destructions and deformities on a country which desired only to be its old quiet, modest, liberal and cultured self.

Not that I believe the true soul of Czechoslovakia can be finally destroyed. 1918, Masaryk, Beneš. 1938, Munich. 1948, Stalin's communist putsch and overthrow. 1968, Russia's invasion and domination. What of 1978 or '88?

9

AFTER MUNICH

After Munich the deluge. Of course Harold Nicolson had been right in what he said, and Karel Capek in what he implied. It was Harold Nicolson's 'six months' almost to a day, it was the 15th of March, the Ides of March, that Hitler, despite his sworn undertaking, marched into Prague and swallowed all the rest of Czechoslovakia. 'There was a certain soothsayer who had given Caesar warning long time afore to take heed of the Ides of March, for on that day he should be in great danger. That day being come, Caesar going into the Senate House and speaking merrily unto the soothsayer told him, "The Ides of March be come." "So be they," answered the soothsayer softly, "but yet are they not past".' There was no merriment in the senate houses and chancelleries of Europe on these Ides of March, 1939. In this hour it became clear that Hitler's rapes and seizures were no longer limited to countries with a German population. His arms were now extended round Poland, a country mainly of Slavs like the Czechs, and Jews; and no one could doubt any more that Poland was next on his list. And after Poland, who? Instantly Great Britain, having learned on that 15th March the full lesson of Munich, gave a guarantee of aid to Poland and its assurance to the world that any further seizure of non-German countries would be met by war.

Even before Munich, when it looked likely to many of us that other countries than Czechoslovakia and Poland were on Hitler's shopping list, and our England might be one of them, I had enrolled as an A.R.P. warden. I might have decided that the policy of a novelist was to be committed to the Eternities, to the things of 'all time' rather than to those of current time, but this was no policy for a citizen of a threatened country, once he had laid down his professional pen and dwelt in the present day. In the heavy, louring, and fetid air of World Fascism neither true humanity nor true art could breathe. And as both writer and citizen one must use the 'magic of the word' (so far as one had acquired any skill in it) in the fight for one's human brothers and one's art. One must write about the right of humans to be humane, and the right of all writers to write. And, to begin with, I would be an air-raid warden.

As wardens we were trained in every branch of Air-Raid Precautions: how to distinguish and deal with the different gas-bombs, or with anything else that might drop from the sky—incendiaries, high-explosives, parachute-mines; how to gas-proof rooms and construct basement or ground-floor refuges which would remain standing after the house fell upon them; what to do at 'incidents'—which was Authority's brutally calm and inadequate word for a building just bombed with its wounded, its dead, and its living lying trapped beneath it; how to give first-aid to the wounded and the buried and the broken when we had recovered them.

But all this was preliminary; presumably war must be declared before the bombs fell; we were but practising. September 1st in '39 was the day when all became real. That morning Hitler's armies invaded Poland, his heavy bombs advancing ahead of them. Immediately, from the opposite direction—behind them—came the British and French ultimatums. And immediately one plan, long prepared, was put into execution. Thousands of children were moved out of London.

Two thousand came into my Sussex town. As a warden I had my allotted duties in this irruption: to take my car to the station where a hundred others would be waiting to receive the children.

Excited, I drove it down to the station, observing on my way how the whole town was dressing itself for war. Shirt-sleeved policemen were building sand-bag walls around the station; post-office men doing the same around their Telephone Exchange; hospital porters and cooks and consultants around the hospital—all, police, postmen, hospitallers being helped by friendly volunteers and delighted children. Soldiers were guarding the station with bayonets fixed. Porters were painting the pavement kerbs white so that they could be seen in a black-out. Other men were painting white stripes around telegraph poles and the trunks of trees.

And here, along our high viaduct, came the first of the children's trains, the children at its windows waving and shouting and singing. Guided by their teachers, they descended to our waiting cars, their packs of clothing on their backs; their gas-masks slung at their sides; and in their school satchels the parcels of food which anxious mothers had given them. Each child had an identity label hung on its breast or sewn there for greater safety. The label sewn on one little girl was half as big as a sandwich-man's board; that child's mother was taking no risks.

The children were shepherded into a spacious, emptied garage, where they were examined by doctors and then given each a day's rations in a paper bag. Boy Scouts were packing these bags from stacks of rations piled against the walls. My car was but one of an endless fleet of residents' cars waiting to take the children to their foster homes, and it was a long time before I was given six of them for my passengers. I had sweets on the dashboard waiting for them but these were hardly necessary since they'd all been given a present of chocolates at the garage.

All that day the trains came rolling over our high bridge, loud with the laughter and cheering of children, and aflower from end to end with waving hands. All that day I took my small passengers to their several homes. Sometimes I carried with them a teacher if they were very young children; and once a pregnant mother whose hour was nearly come. She was already in pain and I could but remember the old Bible words: 'as soon as she is delivered of the child, she remembereth no more the anguish, for joy that a man is born into the world.' *This* world? Only a few of the housewives to whom I brought these children were sullen, resenting this compulsory imposition; most gathered the children in with outstretched hands.

All that night searchlights swept the sky.

This was September 1st. On Sunday the third, at nine in the morning our ambassador in Berlin gave the German Government two further hours to decide upon the withdrawal of their troops from the soil of Poland; if no such decision was reported to us within that time we would be at war. No such answer came; it was eleven o'clock; and war. At a quarter after the hour Chamberlain broadcast to the nation, his fine deep voice weary, sad, and a little hoarse, but his words not ignoble.

'We and France are today, in fulfilment of our obligations, going to the aid of Poland, who is so bravely resisting this wicked and unprovoked attack upon her people. We have a clear conscience. We have done all that a country could do to establish peace. The situation in which no word given by Germany's ruler could be trusted, and no people or country feel themselves safe, has become intolerable. And now we have resolved to finish it. . . . May God bless you all. May he defend the right. It is the evil things we shall be fighting—brute force, bad faith, injustice, oppression and persecution; and against them I am certain that the right will prevail.'

I have to report that, instead of alarm and dismay at these words, something more like pleasure possessed my heart: it was not only pleasure in the excitement and drama which were now come to fill the dullness of our days; this puerile and crude emotion was there; but the chief, leaping pleasure was one of relief: the weight of Munich had been lifted off our conscience.

My passion of indignation could not but invade, to the point of possession, all that I wrote in the days after Munich and the first days of war. Especially it invaded a novel I had begun to write immediately after Munich and continued in '39 and '40. This was written contemporaneously with the events described, which is probably not the best way to write a novel; certainly it cannot then be the product of 'emotion remembered in tranquillity'; but at least, and even though the characters in it were imaginary, it has been a loaded reservoir providing me with immediate 'diary impressions' for the writing of these few chapters of autobiography. The same passion drove me, as passion so often does, to express it, or seek to express it, in poems. One is driven towards this because poems with their high compression, their austere form and their memorable music, have a power acuter and more lasting than any prose. I wrote several poems and of two of them at least, and after all the years, I remain unashamed. One was written within hours of the moment when we declared war on Germany, on that Sunday, September 3rd.

THE FREE PEOPLES RISE

We were late upon our feet because our limbs and wills were free,
And none could make us stand and arm but those who made us see;
But now we see the menace in the quiet summer sky
We stand, the men the ages freed, to order our reply;
We tarried in our standing; so be it; this was best,
For we so free to rise at will shall be the last to rest.
We take our past upon us, and the burden of its fame.
Our past has called its mortgage in, and we shall meet the claim.

The other is perhaps more 'Georgian' and less suited to modern taste, but it held my mood in England's most desperate hour; and I stand by it. It was written, looking out of a train window at an English landscape under an Indian summer sky, in that war autumn of '39, when no one knew what might be upon us at any moment. The whole broad and various pattern of the Sussex Weald lay before me: meadows and hedgerows, beech woods and spires, with the long bare wave of the downs swinging away into a pale blue haze which suggested the sea. The sea and the threat and the Channel ports into England.

I sing no song of England. My wits are slow and dry;
I only rise to help her and, rising, wonder why.
Why beats my heart for England you wiser men may know;
I know this only, brothers: she calls me and I go.

The secret that is England her long green pastures keep;
Her quiet hamlets store it; her hills that seem asleep
Enfold it in the valleys with ploughland, park, and wood.
Her milk-white mists enshroud it, and know that it is good.

These sing the song of England, whose words I cannot hear;
I only know they build for me a meaning that is dear;
They sing perhaps her sage old soul that slowly toils to find
The way to freedom, faithfulness, and laughter that is kind.
Oh, she has sins aplenty, and her broad green breast is scarred,
But the hills that girdle England keep a truth that I shall guard.

10

NOT WANTED

The poem quoted above did express a true and aching desire to serve England in this hour. I felt a more total faith in the justice of her war than ever before (or is this true? Did I not feel much the same in 1914?) and I longed to have a more active and effective role in the fight than my part-time occupation as a somewhat muddle-headed air-raid warden in a country town.

But at the end of 1939 I should be fifty-one, and it seemed therefore that if in my fifties I had anything to offer my country, it must lie in such expertise in the art of words as I might have attained and in such name as I had among readers of my novels and occasional poems. After all, there was old *Tell England* which had now sold some 300,000 copies, and consider: its very title 'Tell England' ought surely to be a quick passport into the Ministry of Information. So, full of hope, I wrote to the Ministry of Information offering to do anything anywhere, in any country, by writing or speaking, to expound our Cause. After a long while—an offensively long while—I received a reply. It said 'Dear Sir or Madam' (*that* put me in my place) 'I regret we have no employment to offer you, and beg to inform you that your application has accordingly been forwarded to the Ministry of Labour.'

And did I hear a word from the Ministry of Labour during five and a half years of war? I did not. It was all very well for me to write, as I looked out of a train window, full of love for England, 'I know this only, brothers: she calls me, and I go.' She did not call me; nor were my brothers the least interested in me; and I had nowhere to go. In the event, as I have told you, the only way I was able, and allowed, to help fight for civilization was as a hopelessly confused lance-corporal in the Home Guard.

This humbling, but maybe healthy, experience reminded me that after the previous war, in 1918, when the politicians or the civil servants were preparing the Demobilization Lists, and grading the boys in the order of their importance to the well-being of the state, Class 1 included 'teachers and miners'. Novelists and poets were in Class 41.

So there was nothing for me to do but to continue as an air-raid warden, and write the book I have referred to above, about Munich and post-Munich and the first days of war, hoping that when published it might play its part, here and there, in fortifying the morale of the people.

Nothing else. That was all. Until six o'clock in the evening of 14th May 1940.

In April 1940 the war, after merely simmering and smoking for seven months, burst into flame with the Germans invading Denmark and Norway; by May it was flaming across Holland, Belgium, and Luxemburg; and when these small countries lay ravished and helpless, it ran over the frontiers of France. All the Channel ports, those 'pistols at the heart of England' were under threat; it looked as if within weeks they must fall.

And at six o'clock on the 14th of May the Secretary of State for War, Mr Anthony Eden, broadcast an appeal for civilian volunteers of any age from seventeen to sixty-five to join a new force which was being organized to deal (this was its first idea) with any enemies landing by parachute or from aeroplanes on our local English fields. The force was to be called 'Local Defence Volunteers'.

Good Mr Eden had never shown any awareness of a magic in words, either to stir emotion or to depress it, and it took a master of the magic, Churchill, to point out to him that 'Local Defence Volunteers' was a sadly costive trio of abstractions and that his new force had much better be called, in three simple stirring words, 'The Home Guard'.

In his broadcast Eden told us that those willing to join his L.D.V. could report to their local police stations next morning.

Enthusiastically resolved to be transformed from a civilian warden to a combatant of sorts I was at our police station after breakfast next morning. I confess I expected some praise for this promptitude, as I passed through the sand-bag barrier that protected the station's doorway. It was not forthcoming. The uniformed policeman behind his desk sighed as he said, 'We can take your name and address. That's all.' A detective-inspector in mufti, whom I knew, explained this absence of any fervour. 'You're about the hundred-and-fiftieth who's come in so far, Mr Raymond, and it's not yet half past nine. Ten per cent of 'em may be some use to Mr Eden but, lor' luv-a-duck, we've had 'em stumping in more or less on crutches. One old codger who we know for a cert is seventy-odd came in and swore he was sixty-one. I said "Make it sixty-two, Charlie," but he said, "No. Sixty-one. Last birthday." And the kids! Gawd-aw' mighty, we've had 'em coming in and swearing they were seventeen last March. We've taken their names but, Gawd's truth, this is going to be Alexander's rag-time army.'

These 'kids' gave me an idea; so infectious is sin. As the policeman at the counter was writing down my name, address, employment, and age I decided to be forty-nine instead of fifty-one—no, forty-seven—forty-nine looked too obvious a fiddle, and, further, if accepted as truth, too near a possible date of discharge. Like most men of middle age—and we are mostly fools—I imagined I looked much younger than I was; so I was written down as forty-seven, and the Inspector, telling me in jest to 'sign the crime-sheet' was nearer the truth than he knew. Or perhaps he knew and forbore in the circumstances to charge me.

As I passed out through the sandbags I met three more volunteers about to file in through the crack. I knew them all. One was an elderly gentleman-farmer who'd brought his sporting gun in the hope, I suppose, that it might fill a gap in the country's armament. Another had his hunting dog with him; but whether it went with him everywhere or he thought, probably correctly, that it would make a wonderful local defence volunteer I don't know. All explained that they were 'joining up like billy-oh', so I prepared them for the worst. I said, 'Well, don't expect any welcome in there. They don't love us. And get it over quickly. I rather suspected that if I stayed around too long, I'd be arrested for loitering.'

Much to the annoyance of my senior warden I contrived my transmutation from an air-raid warden into a local defence volunteer. In outer appearance all that happened was a white brassard on my arm with the letters L.D.V. instead of one with the letters A.R.P. Our local volunteers had been many—over three hundred, I believe; more than the newly appointed Powers could cope with—especially since the only weapons available for us were a dozen old Lee Enfield rifles and our share (six weapons) of outmoded rifles kindly hurried over from America to help Britain save herself. We were split into sections and drilled by an ancient 'dug-out' N.C.O. in a yard behind the Y.M.C.A. hut. Motley sections we were, most of us over fifty and some of us far too fat. In the absence of sufficient rifles we were given flat wooden slabs, cut more or less into a rifle's shape; and with these our old N.C.O. (in a trilby hat) taught us how to slope arms, ground arms, port arms, and even present arms to him, as he walked past us with the port and the hauteur (as he conceived them) of a Commander-in-chief. In the long summer evenings—and what a summer that was in 1940, radiant and calm and ever-unfading over the fields of England—we gambolled about the countryside in extended order and sometimes flung ourselves on to our bellies (though 'flung' is too flattering a word for many of us) so as to practise firing at a deep and wide tank-trap dug across our meadows. We made Molotov cocktails (bottles of inflammable stuff with fuse attached) and Molotov bread-baskets (bundles of incendiaries which exploded on contact). With these amateur bombs we manned road-blocks newly made at the entrances to our town and practised hurling this death at approaching tanks. Once we were allowed to use real Molotovs, tossing them at a derelict car till it was well aflame. We enjoyed that. Hitler, having heard that England now bristled with a million L.D.V.s, civilians all, and not entitled to fight, announced that we should be executed without mercy when the Germans arrived—which delighted us all.

These were days before the L.D.V. were given army ranks and organized as army regiments, and I was soon made responsible for a 'section' and called a 'section leader'. Taking our turns, we patrolled given sectors or stood on guard over crucial places throughout the nights from sun-down to sun-up, lest fifth-columnists acted ahead of invaders. The evening watch was from nine-thirty to one-thirty; the dawn watch from one-thirty to five-thirty. The church of our small town stood on a hill, and its square tower, though squat, commanded from its top a spacious view of the country around. No better 'O.Pip' (observation point) than this, and after the fall of France in June and the enemy occupation of the Channel ports, when invasion seemed likely any day, my section was made responsible for it. We fixed a telephone on its battlemented top, subscribed for by one of our number, Army Signals having refused to erect one of their own instruments, saying they had no authority to do so, and the Post Office having declined to install one of theirs unless some individual undertook to pay the rent. Any of us who possessed field-glasses lent them to my section. One old lady, worried about those noble men on the church tower, insisted on providing a rope-ladder down which they could climb lest the Germans should set the church tower alight (which they were reputed to do, and in our case, as I sometimes think now, would have been justified in doing).

So did Britain begin her warfare against the most magnificently organized army on earth.

One of my section was none other than Christopher Stone, most celebrated of the early disc-jockeys. I used to like having him as my mate on the tower for a night watch, since he always arrived with a camp chair and a hamper, packed with chicken and salad and sandwiches and cakes and bottles of wine—on a good night champagne—that the length of the night might be made tolerable. He brought also a hamper of good stories (in the form of his fine head) about Eton and his famous father, the Rev. E. D. Stone, a master at Eton; about Oxford and the House and the First War (where he won both a D.S.O. and an M.C.) and the B.B.C. and the Beefsteak Club; and about his famous brother-in-law Compton Mackenzie. If Compton Mackenzie is the best raconteur in Britain—and I suspect he is—Christopher Stone was probably his runner-up. At least I should regard him as one of the seeded players in the game. I remember tracts of the long night under the stars—never any rain that wonderful summer—when, instead of being behind my binoculars and sweeping the broad landscape for parachutists I was guiltily seated, shaking with laughter at his stories as I drank his wine or shared his chicken, while the rolling green fields of Sussex lay open to the enemy. One householder near the church complained that our voices and laughter kept him awake and, as commander of the section, I was instructed that this manner of laughing up there 'must cease forthwith'. Christopher Stone's proper place from which to broadcast comedy was a B.B.C. studio, not the top of our church tower in war time.

§

As daily the invasion seemed more likely and imminent I got my son home from Dartington, his school, and like other parents, blind to what might be coming, sent him as far from England as possible. With one of his schoolfellows he went to South Africa. Some of my friends sent their children to America; others to Australia and New Zealand. I find that to many people now, though they know most about the Second World War, it is a surprise to learn that in 1940 British middle-class children were distributed by their parents all over the world.

I myself, driven by my appetite for excitement and drama, to say nothing of a novelist's desire for tremendous topics as 'copy', left Sussex and took a furnished flat in Hampstead—quite simply, and since I was 'not wanted' by Britain in any specialist capacity—that I might see her war at its centre in London. This desire for excitement and drama has always been stronger in me than the fear of danger; it smothers the fear almost into unconsciousness, even though no one dislikes pain more than I. The excitement, the drama, of a menacing disaster can even smother, for a moment, both horror and compassion. The battle for freedom, with London for its great Headquarters, and as the enemy's principal target, would be, for sure, the greatest event in our history since the Conquest, and I was resolved to see the very heart of it. London housing the exiled governments of Europe's stolen countries, with their kings or queens and their officers and men of their Armies of Liberation would be the capital, not only of Great Britain, but of the Free World Fighting.

And in all London there was no better flat than this new one of mine from which to see her war. It was a top flat in Church Row, Hampstead, and since the summit-ridge of London's Northern Heights (Hampstead and Highgate) is 417 feet above sea-level, or 17 feet above the cross on the dome of St Paul's, and since this top flat was in a fairly tall block facing south, it overlooked the whole capital under its silver barrage balloons, and all the Thames Valley as far as the grey swaying hills of Surrey and Kent.

It was here that Diana Young, first met at the Young P.E.N., came to me and we joined our lives together.

Zoë, my first wife, and I, though we had always been good friends, and she was a gifted home-maker, had failed, in one or two ways, to make a full success of our marriage. We had resolved, however, to remain together till our two children were much older and nearer to some settlement in life; and we did, in fact, live in a very fair relationship for 18 years. In 1940 my son Patrick was, as I have told, in South Africa and likely to remain there for the war's duration (though actually when he was old enough to serve he returned home to join the R.A.F., in which he is now a Wing-Commander). My daughter, Lella, a convert to Roman Catholicism, was about to embark on the valuable wartime work of nursing, a profession to which she has since devoted her life.

So Diana and I married; and this high flat was our first home. We had been there for but a few weeks when it was Saturday, September 7th, 1940, one of the few war dates fixed in our minds for ever. And not the date only, but one hour of it: about five o'clock on that September Saturday. It is early evening, and still daylight. Suddenly the sound of bombs. Heavy bombs falling in the distance. And instantly the angry response of London's anti-aircraft guns which always lifted one's heart —or mine, at any rate—into irrational transports of appreciation. The haughty, mighty, furious voice of London. We hurried to our wide front window, and there, far to the south-east where Dockland lay north and south of the river, the black smoke-clouds were rising and the sky above them was a red glare reflecting flames from buildings ablaze. We imagined it to be no more than a new raid, though the biggest yet, directed at the docks. In fact the blitzkrieg on London had begun. The Dockland conflagrations made a glowing map-reference for relay after relay of bombers on this first night of the 'Blitz'; and we stood for an hour at our window watching Dockland and its surroundings in south-east London burn.

That night we had tickets for the theatre, for *Abraham Lincoln* at the Westminster; and since the bombing was at least eight miles from Hampstead and probably five from Princes Row where our theatre was, we were not disposed to lose the advantage of our tickets. So in that little theatre we watched a play about another war, while hearing through its walls the muffled detonations of bombs and the gloriously infuriated, indignant, insulted barrage from London's guns. All this continued throughout the performance because it was at eight o'clock and in the first dark that the raiders came in their greatest force. Eight o'clock was the true beginning. But the theatre's manager had come before the curtains and said 'Ladies and gentlemen, our play will proceed as announced without regard to these irrelevances without'—a statement greeted with cheers and laughter and applause.

In the interval we left our seats and went out on to the pavement to see how the night was faring. Little black-out in the streets that night because the sky was on fire. And this unnatural light was ever illuminated by stronger lights within it, the flashes of our guns. There was a terrible luminous beauty about that night in London marred by a smell as of burnt oil from the tanks and reservoirs of Dockland.

When the play was over, closing with its brief tribute-line to a great war leader, 'Now he belongs to the ages', and when the cast had been given a furore of cheers, Diana and I came out into streets still aglow from the fires, and, needing food, went to the Windsor Dive by Victoria Station. Here we found a happy congregation of people feeding from high stools at the counters or at the tables and making merry over the events of the night.

These events were still in progress. This opening act of the London Blitz lasted from five that evening to five the next morning. The ensuing acts, raining H.E. bombs, incendiaries, and parachute mines promiscuously all over London, lasted through September, October, November, and part of December, nearly ninety nights in all. It is strange to remember that in every one of those ninety nights Diana and I slept, and slept well enough, in our top-floor room with little but the slates between us and our German visitors, and while all the guns encircling London tore up the night with their roaring and blasting and thunder-cracks. There was a 'shelter' of sorts on the ground-floor of our flats, but we both decided that if a bomb crashed through our block and destroyed it, we'd rather go down with the building than have the building come down on us. The one fear in me which no excitement could easily smother was a horror of being buried alive. My agent, W. P. Watt, once asked me how I was getting on beneath it all in a top-flat, and I told him, 'I'm loving it. When a bomb drops near us the whole building sways, and all our landlord's brass ornaments topple from the mantel-shelf to the floor, Diana flings her arms round me for safety, and I feel like the Rock of Ages.' He replied with his usual poker-faced humour, 'I should feel like a broken reed.'

I have a good friend today, Ian Norrie, who is not only a gifted book-seller (his friends say 'one of the best in London') but has created his own publishing house, 'High Hill Bookshops, Ltd' (the 'high hill' being Hampstead's steep hill) and published among other books two symposia on our Northern Heights. One is *The Book of Hampstead* and the other, *The Heathside Book*. I contributed to the first, my wife to the second. He lets me quote from them liberally, and I will pilfer first from my wife's because it deals with the Blitz.

She called it *Winter Scene with Bombs* and here are two passages from it which may recall much to many and tell something to those who in '40 were children or unborn. She was working at the Ministry of Food and would return by the Underground to Hampstead.

'There are strange memories of the Tube. Hampstead is the deepest station in London, two hundred feet down and when the nightly raids established themselves after that Saturday in September, the people came there steadily, with babies and food and bedding; and the ruling that the Tubes were not to be used as shelters had to go down before them. From early in the afternoon they could be seen pushing perambu-lators, going purposefully towards the station, where they waited in line till six o'clock when they were allowed on the platforms. The long queues grew longer as the dark came down earlier and the raids lasted from dusk to dawn.

'Those were the early days before the Tube shelters were organized, before bunks were built and sanitary arrangements provided. Now, not in panic, but in a determination for safety, the people came and lay on the ground, heads against the tiled wall. They lay on the platforms, in the corridors, and on the stairs. At night, coming home on the Tube, one stepped into another world. The huddled, weary figures pressed close together and wrapped in blankets, the stench of sweat and urine, conveyed the air of a civilization crumbled, of a world stepping backward in time and order. Late at night the close-packed figures were largely silent. A baby cried; there was a sound of snoring in the sour, heavy air; here and there one saw a woman propped against the tiled wall, awake, staring at nothing; perhaps with some memory of destruction and death. One picked one's way over the bodies and round the children, finding a path; at the top was the dark, menacing, but clean air, and the dubious but more comfortable sanctuary of a top flat in Church Row. . . .

'One morning that winter the taps in Church Row gave only a few grudging drops; then nothing but a kind of asthmatic snoring, usually associated in one's mind with going under gas. (This emergency was probably caused, the Metropolitan Water Board tell me, by damage to the 48-inch and 42-inch mains.) Bearing pails, saucepans and jugs, we went out into the street, my husband, myself, and Mrs Warren who faithfully surfaced every morning, after sleeping in Camden Town tube station, to work for us all through the Blitz.

'In Church Row we found numbers of people, also carrying jugs, pails, and anything that would hold water. Rumours drifted this way and that; water diviners were at a premium. A stand-pipe attached to a main under the pavement by the church ran out (one's pessimism would say "inevitably") before our turn came. We turned back into Church Row. Out of one of the graceful eighteenth-century houses a distinguished-looking gentleman emerged, wearing the dignified morning-dress of happier times and carrying a pail. "There's some in Flask Walk," he called to us pleasantly. "But," he added, "you can't drink it." This became evident when, at the end of Flask Walk, we found a large tank of stagnant water, an emergency supply for the fire services, its surface covered with slime, leaves, and refuse. But it would do, Mrs Warren said, for the floors. On arriving back in Church Row, we found two camouflaged R.A.S.C. lorries, loaded with milk-churns of water, parked against the kerb. We went upstairs to tell Mrs Warren, who had gone ahead of us, that the Army had taken over and Hampstead was saved.'

§

One more comment I must quote from *Winter Scene with Bombs*. It runs: 'That winter the doctor said, "You may expect your baby at the end of May." In the light of all else one could expect before then it seemed a statement of some optimism.' I quote it because it was in this context that there happened the most sensational thing in my life—I used the word 'sensational' because the newspapers were calling it a 'sensation' all over the world, my young son in South Africa even reading it with a personal interest. I was not the subject of the sensation, nor Diana, but our four-day-old son was.

The child was born on 1st June 1941, in the Woolavington Wing of the Middlesex Hospital. A nurse brought him in, wrapped in a shawl, to show him to Diana who had been barely conscious during the birth. He was a fine boy, weighing eight and a quarter pounds, certainly a baby to be proud of, but Diana, though not troubled, was surprised by a slight yellowness in his complexion.

'Don't mind that,' said the nurse. 'That's nothing to worry about. New-born babies are often jaundiced.'

So Diana—and I too when, next day, I was allowed to see the child—remained proud.

But that same day, while I was in my wife's room, the child having been taken to the infants' ward, a staff-nurse came in and said to me—notably to me alone—'Can I have a word with you, please?'

I said Yes; but she motioned me to come out into the corridor. Naturally these words and movements left Diana in a grip of anxiety and fear. For a minute and more that seemed an hour.

On my re-entering the room, she asked, 'What is it? What is it?'

And I had to tell her, 'They don't like the jaundice now. It's getting worse, and—I can't quite understand what it's all about—but they're ... a little afraid.'

Soon the nurse was followed by the Gynaecological Registrar who gently and sympathetically explained to us that the jaundice was a rare and serious form. He gave us its Latin name, *Icterus gravis neonatorum*.

Gravis?

Yes, the outlook in such cases was always grave. But all that the hospital could do, it would do.

Following him out into the corridor I asked, Did he mean that it could be fatal.

Frankly, out of Diana's hearing, he allowed that this was possible. 'But the hospital will do all it can.'

And I had not been long back in Diana's room when a sister entered and called me out again.

A religious woman, she said, 'Don't you think the baby had best be baptized at once? The chaplain is ready to do it.'

'If you think so,' I said.

And the child was taken down to the hospital's little chapel and baptized, the sister and I alone watching.

§

Icterus gravis neonaytorum: grave jaundice of the new-born.

So far as an ignorant layman can define the condition, it is this. In 1940, only a year before our son was born, an American scientist discovered that there could be a factor in the red blood cells of human beings which he named the 'Rh-factor' because the same factor always occurs in the blood of the Indian Rhesus monkey. About eighty-five per cent of humans have this Rh-factor and are therefore called 'Rhesus-positive'; the remaining minority of fifteen per cent lack it and so are called 'Rhesus-negative'. It was at once ascertained in the hospital that my wife was 'Rhesus-negative' and I 'Rhesus-positive'. Let me here—with relief—quote from an article by Lord Ritchie-Calder who really understands all about the 'Rh'—as indeed about all other scientific matters under the sun. 'An Rh-negative mother,' he says, 'can have a baby which inherits an Rh-positive from its father. Sometimes the Rh-factor from the unborn baby's blood invades the mother's blood-stream. Hostile antibodies are then created to resist the invasion, and these in turn pass into the blood-stream of the baby, working havoc with its Rh-positive blood corpuscles. As a result the baby may be still-born or born with jaundice or fatal anaemia.'

Thus, as Lord Ritchie-Calder pointed out, there can arise 'the heart-breaking circumstance that a perfectly healthy and loving mother is destroying her own child'.

Nowadays such babies are usually saved by a complete transfusion of new blood. Not so in 1941 when there was still much to learn about the Rh-factor. 1941; the Germans were in command of all the Channel ports; France's Vichy government was supporting them; invasion was still a possibility; all our coasts were watched by regular troops and Home Guards; concrete blockhouses and strongpoints stood in the London streets ready to enfilade them; all Britain wondered what the summer would hold—and yet, it will always be an overwhelming memory to Diana and myself, that, as it seemed to us, the Middlesex Hospital, one of London's greatest teaching hospitals, turned inward with any number of its consultants, doctors, sisters and students, studying how 'Baby Raymond' could be saved. So little was the Rh-factor understood in '41 that at first the hospital was giving the child, through one arm and both ankles, transfusions of its mother's blood—the one thing, I imagine, that was a complete mistake—and rapidly the child's condition deteriorated. The 'blood count' went down and down —that is to say the red blood corpuscles were being steadily broken down, and the child was becoming drowsy. But then, on the third day, the child, Peter, being still only seventy-five hours old, Sir Alfred Webb-Johnson, later Lord Webb-Johnson and President of the Royal College of Surgeons, came into Diana's room with an entourage of doctors, sisters and nurses, and in his kindliest voice said to us both, 'You have an enormously bonny baby, but'—turning to Diana—'there's only one thing wrong with him, my dear, and we think that if you will let me operate on him we can save him.'

They had decided that the best thing to do was to remove the spleen —the spleen being a seat in the body where the red blood corpuscles multiply and are most easily destroyed, thereby increasing the jaundice and the danger of a fatal issue. Research, especially among the students, had shown that though this had never been done in England, it had been tried in America and had succeeded. 'If you and your husband will consent,' Lord Webb-Johnson said to us, 'I will operate at once.'

What could we do but consent and thank him? With an encouraging smile he went out with his retinue and our son was taken straight to the operating theatre.

Let me now hand the story over to *The Lancet*.

The Lancet's report on the operation says, 'In consultation with Sir Alfred Webb-Johnson splenectomy was decided upon and this was performed at 7 p.m. on June 4th when the baby was seventy-five hours old. General anaesthesia with gas oxygen and ether was used, and the operation was completed within twenty minutes. Feeding was commenced four hours later and a three-hour regime was resumed in twenty-four hours—' how well we remember Peter being brought in after the operation, smelling powerfully of the anaesthetic, one arm in a splint because of the blood transfusions and his skin still as yellow as an orange. Apparently he was not uninterested in a meal, and in the next few days I took to calling him 'a milk hound'. *The Lancet* article continues, 'Blood counts an hour and fourteen hours after operation showed that the fall in the red cells and haemoglobin had been arrested and a response was beginning.'

Every paper in Britain, including the small local journals, told the story—some in sensational terms, the *Mirror*'s headline being 'Miracle of Surgery for Baby's Life'; its story calling it 'a wonder operation never before attempted in this country on one so young'. Lord Webb-Johnson told me afterwards that the work of the anaesthetist was indeed wonderful, and that, on the whole, he himself was more proud of this operation than of any other he had performed. Never shall I forget the day when a staff-nurse rushed into my wife's room and cried excitedly, 'The blood-count's gone up! The blood-count's gone up!' The Gynaecological Registrar, Oswald Lloyd, followed her to say 'Gosh, that baby of yours must be a tough egg. He didn't turn a hair, and now the blood-count's going up!' Thereafter, through five weeks, optimism succeeded upon optimism. And the last words of *The Lancet*'s article are: 'Convalescence was prolonged by slight infection of the lower end of the wound, but the baby was discharged fit and well on July 5th fully breast-fed.' The *Daily Mail* seized on this, and with Fleet Street's normal dislike of understatement, celebrated the story with the headline, 'Peter at a Month Old is Famous'.

I repeat that this great hospital gave much of itself to a new-born child while Germany stood massed at the gates of Britain.

11

HAMPSTEAD MOUNTS HER GUARD

On leaving my Sussex home to live in London and see the war, I got myself transferred to the Hampstead Home Guard, and at some time before or after Peter's operation (I forget when) the Home Guard became part of the Army instead of civilian volunteers. Our Hampstead Home Guard was now a unit of a famous regiment: we were No. 15 Company of the 20th Middlesex Regiment and, along with others of the rank and file, 'Volunteer Raymond' became 'Private Raymond'. After a while I attained the rank of Lance-Corporal, on which dizzy eminence I remained for the rest of the war. But I have always been prouder of my single lance-corporal's stripe than I was of my three stars in the First War. These were just granted to me gratuitously on being commissioned, the Army being indisposed for their spiritual directors who must take command of church parades to have less than a captain's rank. My single stripe in the Home Guard was not a concession: was it not earned by the sweat of a middle-aged brow? It most certainly was. So now I will quote, with Ian Norrie's permission, from my article in his *Book of Hampstead*. It is called *An Old Platoon* and was written fifteen years after the war's end.

'Last evening, for the purposes of this essay I walked across the many undulations of Hampstead Heath and into those haunted places which were once the fields and farmlands and the noble landscaped park of Kenwood House, the "Great Lord Mansfield's" eighteenth-century home. And time and again as I walked in those fields and the park my eyes sought the ground for I was looking for a lost and buried history; for me, quite literally, a buried treasure, because it was now underground and the grass grew over it, and it was made up of rich memories.

'Let me explain. Once there was a queer fraternity of men in Hampstead, mostly middle-aged or worse, who had volunteered for an important task with the usual British mixture of flippancy, cynical self-ridicule and an adequate flavour of pungent grumbling. They were drawn from every class, party, religion, profession and trade—even from more than one nationality. I remember amongst them lawyers, civil servants, bank clerks, big businessmen and small shop-keepers; an editor, a publisher, a labourer and a verger. In full service uniform (at last) they came to be called No. 15 Company, Home Guard, and their task was nothing less than to defend Hampstead from any airborne enemy that "dared to invade the borders of their realm". Since I was but a rank-and-file unit in "No. 1 Platoon", it is only of this particular brotherhood that I can speak with any assurance that I am talking truth and sense (so obscure are his military performances to a mere ranker).

'When a German invasion of England still seemed a likely affair, say in 1940 and '41, it was plain that the great open spaces which are the glory of Hampstead—the Heath, Kenwood Fields, Kenwood Park, Parliament Fields, Golders Hill Park—were possible landing grounds for parachute and airborne troops during an attempted attack on London. With any such insolent operation our No. 15 Company was trained and equipped—and eager—to interfere. Every one of those open spaces was for us a field of fire. On a dozen rises and ridges slit trenches were sited for us by the Brigade of Guards (who should know their job but of course the old sweats among us bitterly criticized their siting) and from these grave-like trenches we were prepared to sweep all the areas before us with a cross-fire, so that few, if any, of our visitors would escape these killing-grounds. If any did escape, say into the cover of Ken Wood itself, why then we had our mobile reserve to beat the wood, find them, and deal with them there.

'That was our tactical task, and it was the sites of these old slit trenches that I went looking for last evening. They were long ago filled up, of course, but was I wrong in thinking that the texture of the grass above them was richer and greener than elsewhere because the earth below had been so deeply disturbed?

'First I looked for that one which used to be just beneath the lovely old dairy and brewhouse of Lord Mansfield's farm, a trench or fire-point which covered all the long grassy slope between dairy and wood; then that which was just under the terrace of the great house and turned its back on Robert Adam's Ionic pilasters so that it could sweep with fire all of Lord Mansfield's landscaped view from his Orangery, Parlour, and Library. Then I went to the one on the western slope which was to send its enfilading cross-fire parallel to house and wood. It was a hot summer evening and all the lawns were burnt into buffs and fawns but the grass above this site was oddly green and shaped like the shadow of a trench. Lastly I went to the one which had most fascination for me since it was my own trench. This was on the ridge between the Old Kitchen Garden and Millfield Lane where once walked Coleridge and

Keats. It covered the view which might, just possibly, have been my last sight of England.

'Well, it is a happy thing that those trenches are now dead and buried and have no existence except in the memories of some elderly gentlemen still at large in our borough or now scattered far from it. It was a good thing, no doubt, to see in the warmth of yesterday evening, people seated in hammock chairs across the very mouths of those trenches or young lovers entwined beside them. . . .

'To those of us who had our place in the H.G. battle squads it is a strange thought that nowadays there must be young men and women who hardly know, or can hardly believe, that there was a time when almost every fit middle-aged man, whatever his profession or trade, had his rifle in a corner, and his battle-dress and equipment hanging on a hook with fifty rounds of ammunition in the pouches.

'This was to be the method of summoning us to battle. Our Platoon Headquarters was in Queen Mary's Maternity Home at the top of Heath Street, which had been evacuated of its mothers and mothers-to-be and was now shared by us with the National Fire Service. On the first warning of the distant approach of troop-carrying aeroplanes a code word shot to the Guard Commander in the Maternity Home; he instantly telephoned it to seven Home Guards in well-placed Hampstead homes; and they thereupon delivered the call, each to a selected list of his fellows or by dashing out and bashing on their doors. It is to be hoped that, had the true summons ever come (we had plenty of practice-calls) we should have been in our trenches or at our Action Stations (if a bit sweaty and unbuttoned) in time to entertain our visitors.

'But I don't know. . . .

'Once the likelihood of a large-scale invasion had been more or less discounted, in '42 and '43, those old trenches were abandoned to the rain and we turned to practising street-fighting, open warfare, and unarmed combat because we were now a tactical reserve ready to reinforce the defences on our northern perimeter of London.'

No quicker impression of Britain's Home Guard in her heroic days, 1940–45, can be provided than the following story. One of our tasks after we'd abandoned the slit trenches was to practise 'night operations', marching with feline tread, in Indian file or extended order, along the streets or across the Heath. Our faces were blackened so as to be invisible in the darkness and no sound escaped from us except a whispering silence. Once a regular officer, of high seniority, came to lecture us on such operations, and he stressed that we must blacken, not only our faces but our teeth: 'Teeth become easily visible in the dark,' he was explaining, when our O.C., Major Coltman (only 'Lieutenant' in the Home Guard) intervened to remind him, 'But, sir, Home Guards don't need to blacken their teeth. They just take them out.'

Of course we were not composed only of middle-aged men lacking their complement of teeth; there were young men among us from reserved occupations; but the majority of us were well over military age, and a majority of this majority had the girth and weight natural to their years. However, so constituted, we did our best. I was more fortunate than some because, though in my fifties, I was thin rather than stout. Even so, I remember having to wriggle forward on my stomach over the green hills above the Vale of Health, dragging through the grass a heavy Lewis gun to our field of fire. I arrived safely at our map-reference, with my gun intact but with little breath in my body. It is gratifying to report that none of our more fat and elderly members dropped at any time dead on the Heath. In other parts of the country one or two did, I believe.

We did our best but remained amateur soldiers or rusty and paunched veterans. In those days there was a deep sand-pit or quarry beside the road that runs across the east heath, and this served well as our rifle range, its high rear-cliff of sand behind the targets being a safe wall to receive our bullets. At least that was the plan and the purpose. But one summer evening one of our number was advancing with his rifle to the stop where he must lie prone and take aim. He handled the rifle amateurishly, with its barrel pointing anywhere and a finger touching the trigger. In a moment of abstraction—or apprehension—that finger drew on the trigger while he was still walking, and a bullet shot high into the sky and over the trees of Ken Wood.

We kept quiet about this misadventure, in the hope that no one had died. We estimated that if anyone had been hit and was now wounded or dead, it must have been somewhere in Hampstead Lane on the far side of Kenwood House. Some civilian coming home, maybe.

No such 'incident' was reported, and we thanked the wide Heaven above us for the dim green vastness of the Heath, so capable of absorbing a stray bullet.

That sand-pit or deep quarry is no longer to be seen by people crossing the Heath. It was used as a pit into which heaps of London could be dumped—that is to say cartloads and cartloads of the fragments, rubble, and detritus of bombed London. Soon it was filled up till it was level with the sandy road. The self-sown grass has long grown over it, and when on Bank Holidays the Hampstead Fair is there, no one in the dodgem cars or on the roundabouts knows that he is making whoopee over the grave of much that was London.

One Sunday we paraded at the Maternity Home and Major Coltman marched us two miles and more to the outskirts of Primrose Hill, and so to the Regent's Park Barracks in Albany Street. By the time we arrived at the barracks we had learned, marching at ease, what this curious move portended. There was a Guards battalion quartered in the barracks, and our drilling was to be 'smartened up' by the interposing of smart young guardsmen at various points in our ranks. Their perfectly executed response to every order would demonstrate to us how slow or how clumsy were our reactions. We were divided into squads on the barrack square and each squad was to be drilled by a Guards sergeant-major. The company-sergeant-major who drilled the squad which held me was as typical of his alarming rank as you can imagine: a six-foot, square-shouldered, deep-chested man in a uniform that left the word 'smart' trailing far behind as a weak and inadequate thing. He had a swagger cane under his arm and a voice in his throat which, when necessary, was like that of Jove himself, or perhaps of Mars, the god of war. In his eyes ('like Mars to threaten or command') there was a hint—just a hint—of joviality, as if fun were to be enjoyed this morning, since Home Guards approximated, surely, to figures of fun.

He began by saying, 'Now don't you men imagine that these lads mixed up among you are the smartest boys in the Guards, put there to shame you. They are some of the lousiest we've got—we've picked them as the lousiest. On the whole they are the most slow, awkward and slovenly in the battalion, so if you can't do better than they can, God help you, you've a lot to learn Squad SHUN!'

None of us were ready for that 'Shun!' so we were humiliated at the outset. All the young men 'shunned' two seconds before the best of us did, and three seconds before the rest.

And so it went on through the morning on that barrack square. He put us at the double, bellowed 'HALT!' and the young men halted so suddenly that most of us bumped into the backs of the ram-rod stiff guardsmen in front of us. Was there a guardsman dismayed? Not though the soldier knew Some one had blundered. (I am tempted to

Rabindranath Tagore, Canada, 1929

The Padre's Last Appeal
from L to R in water: Arthur Hardy, Monty Banks, Ellaline
Terriss, Franklin Dyall, Donald Calthrop, Francis Lister

Diana Raymond, *née* Young

Author demonstrating state of Coleridge's tomb

The new coffins of Coleridge and his wife in the floodlit crypt

Brandhoek

The Menin Gate Memorial, with the British lion watching over
the whole of the Ypres Salient. The new spire of Paschendaele
is in the distance.

Rev. W. R. Bi

On the summit of Cam Crag. Seated: Author and Gloria
Guinness. Standing: Maurice Guinness, Sandy, Diana Raymond
and Alwyn Walford

Pamela Chandler

'Pamela'

go on and write, Theirs not to mumble 'Hell!' Theirs but to stand up
well, Theirs not to turn and see who fell—but to remain stiffly vertical,
with eyes front and heads erect, as guardsmen should.)

There was trouble when all too suddenly the sergeant-major yelled
'Right TURN!' and then all too unexpectedly (damn him for a trickster)
'Left TURN!' I am one of those ill-equipped people who have no instant
knowledge which is my right side and which my left. Addressed at
pistol point I sometimes have to think, 'Wait, which hand is it that holds
the knife?' and so I was conspicuously bad on this occasion. More than
once I found myself face to face with a young guardsman who'd turned
the right way. There he stood before me, head erect, shoulders back, and
with no unmilitary grin at his lips—but one behind his eyes. I swore,
turned my back on him, and faced, amid some ridicule, the same way as
he. Face to face, on second thoughts, with Truth.

When we'd finished our morning's drill the sergeant-major said,
'Magnificent. Couldn't be better. Marvellous the way you've shown
these lads how to drill. I hope they feel properly ashamed of themselves,
and you as proud of yourselves as you're entitled to be Squad DIS-
MISS!'

I doubt whether, in spite of all this, our response to that 'Dismiss!'
was any more simultaneous than our movements on his first 'Shun!'
Perhaps it was a shade better, if only because this time it was less unexpected.

At one time we were put through a course on 'Unarmed Combat',
and very brutal our instructions were. The sergeant who was lecturing
us faithfully reproduced the type of those officers in the First War
whom I have always recalled with doubt and distaste, the apostles of
'The Offensive Spirit'. This gospel preached in the latter years of
that war amounted to little less than dealing with our enemies in a
spirit of merciless and murderous 'frightfulness'. We were to drive
the bayonet home and when our man was down stamp on him and twist
the bayonet in his breast before drawing out. 'It's my business,' said
these instructors proudly, 'to turn you into bloody murderers, nothing
less.'

Our 'Unarmed Combat' sergeant was just such another; he gloried
in being 'tough'. Possibly the foul and terrible blows he taught us might
be useful and necessary in an extremity, but what sickened me was the
mood in which he surrounded them. It was the mood of 'If you take my
advice you'll take no prisoners. The only good German is a dead

German.' It was the mood of 'In street fighting if Jerry has got into a house, don't stand hesitating in case there are civilians there, let him have your bombs through every window. We've got to win this war at whatever cost. We've got to equal the Hun in his frightfulness and, if possible, surpass him.' It was the mood which produced the ghastly belief in Saturation Bombing, which issued in our total destruction of Dresden, killing and wounding, according to the lowest estimate 25,000 people; and at last in those hardly speakable actions: Hiroshima and Nagasaki.

'My job is to make you all bloody murderers,' said our sergeant in the old familiar words. He said them in a room which had been a ward of the Maternity Home, a place built for, and consecrated to, help in pain and the preservation of life, where we stood paraded before him. 'And I'm bloody well going to do it. For instance, when you've overcome your man, *this*—' and he illustrated a quick lethal blow. 'Don't just arrest him. He's better dead, less nuisance, ha, ha, ha.' This to an audience of bank clerks, civil servants, shopkeepers and so on. One, an author, after a time could take no more of it. As this lust for savagery illuminated the sergeant's chatter and demonstrations I fretted to argue with him. Of course this was war, in which at times one must kill or be killed, but none the less I had no use for those who rejoiced in being 'tough' for its own sake, because 'toughness' in the minds of such people nearly always meant a contempt for half the things my heart and mind believed in, no matter how poor my practice of them: compassion, humaneness, the abandonment, wherever possible, of retaliatory violence, and the certainty that, in the end, evil can be overcome only by its opposite. In war or out of it they would probably call such ideas sloppy and weak and sentimental. One day perhaps they would understand, though I doubted if they ever would, that it requires far greater strength to be tender than to be tough, because it militates against one's natural drives towards anger, vindictiveness and instant punishment.

At last, so warmed up was I that I cared not what the consequences might be for me as a man standing there in His Majesty's uniform and under military discipline. I began, 'Sergeant?'

'Yes?' he said, thrown off his stride by an unexpected and unmilitary interruption from the ranks.

'What happens, Sergeant,' I asked with a slight trembling of the heart, half exasperation, half fear, which I was glad was invisible, 'to a Home Guard who declines to do some of the things you are advocating?'

'What?' he said again; and had no more to say because he didn't know the answer. In a physical struggle with this expert, I'd have been on the floor in half a breath, but it was plain that, verbally, I'd put him on the floor.

So I took my opportunity and went on, my head having cooled and my heart steadied, 'Is there not a risk here of giving orders which some of us will not be ready to obey? Personally, I didn't join the Home Guard to do some of these things.'

Our good O.C., Major Coltman, was looking non-plussed by this murmur, as of insubordination, in his ranks, but his look, I thought, was not devoid of sympathy—and amusement. He is a witty man. He did not speak, and the sergeant who had now arrived at some sort of answer, held the floor. 'What happens to a Home Guard I don't know,' he said—and in this I suspect he was no different from the Highest Brass in the War Office—'but I can promise you that in the Army you'd be arrested and court-martialled.'

'But we *are* the Army, aren't we: No. 15 Company, 20th Middlesex Regiment?' I submitted, now sweetly reasonable.

'Yes, I suppose you are,' he said, but could add no more, in his enduring confusion.

So the 'parole' was mine, and I was glad to be able to continue with what was simmering in my mind (we all like to finish what we're trying to say): 'I must suggest, Sergeant, that if we are only able to win the war by adopting all the things we have condemned in the Nazis, we may win it materially but they will have won it spiritually.'

I think I knew what I meant then, but I'm sure the sergeant didn't. He just lifted his shoulders and left this difficult proposition in the air. Nor, I fancy, was anyone in the ranks quite clear on my point, though I'd had an alerted and attentive audience throughout this altercation. The O.C., since this brief debate appeared over, just said with a mischievous smile, 'Well, carry on, Sergeant.'

And that was the last I heard of this mutinous murmur in a maternity ward. I imagine that strictly, and in accordance with the Army Act, I was chargeable with threatening 'disobedience of a lawful command given by a superior officer' or, at the least, with 'conduct to the prejudice of good order and military discipline', but I interpret the absence of any action against me as a further illustration of the amateurish, hybrid, half-time quality of Britain's Home Guard. I don't believe that from its creation in 1940 to its demise in 1944 anybody in the War

Office, preoccupied with winning the war on the continent and on the High Seas, had time to work out what exactly we were.

§

All these exercises changed when the Allies' invasion of Normandy was really in train. Then on each duty night we had to sleep in full service order, our weapons at our sides, on the hard floor of the evacuated Biology Library of King Alfred School, ready to awake at call and dash out should efforts be made to disrupt our lines of communication or sabotage important centres by suicide parachute troops or perhaps fifth-column elements.

Good exciting nights and days these were, and it was not without a savour of sorrow that we learned towards the end of '44 that our task was done, and the code word had gone out for the Stand Down. The Stand Down was to be completed by the last day of that year, and our No. 15 Company stood down on Sunday, December 3rd, after a final parade and march-past, saluted gratefully by the Mayors of Hampstead and Hendon.

It was a fine march-past watched by large crowds and marred by only one small mistake. Our officer-in-command, Lieutenant O. P. Milne, later himself a Mayor of Hampstead, bellowed the command 'Eyes *right*!' as we passed the mayors, but forgot for ever after to change it to 'Eyes *front*!' so, presumably, the Hampstead Home Guard marched the next mile or so out of military into civil life with their eyes fixed permanently to the right.

On the Sunday after this farewell march-past we handed in at the Maternity Home our rifles, ammunition, and army boots but were allowed to keep our khaki uniforms either as a souvenir or for work at peace in the garden.

12

PEACE AND A MEDITATION

Five months after this last Dismiss of the Home Guard came V.E. Day, Victory in Europe Day, May 8th. The morning before, at 2.41 a.m., General Jodl, representing the German High Command, signed the act of unconditional surrender of all German land, sea, and air forces, and on May 10th Field Marshal Keitel signed, in Berlin, the ratification of this surrender. Did Jodl and Keitel know, as they wrote their signatures, that they were signing their own death-warrants; that they would later be arrested, put on trial as war-criminals at Nuremberg, sentenced to death, and hanged?

Japan was still at war with us but on an August day the first atom bomb in history fell on Hiroshima, destroying in one burst seven square miles of the city, and killing or mutilating, according to the Japanese official estimate, 138,000. Three more days and a second such bomb fell on Nagasaki, a city of 250,000 people, 'which', said one paper, seemingly with pride, 'had in all probability been wiped off the face of the earth'.

Japan surrendered. A second World War was over.

'Sleep after toil, port after stormy seas, ease after war—' it was peace, and we rejoiced in it, forgetting for a time a voice out of the far past, which cried aloud some twenty-five centuries ago, 'Thus were they defiled with their own works, And went a whoring with their own inventions'; peace, and we left aside for a while the troubling thought that perhaps 'they who take the atom-sword shall perish with the atom-sword'.

In this peace-time quiet I have a fancy to devote a whole chapter to a meditation on the art of the novel. Novelist after novelist, from the austere Master, Henry James himself, has mused before the world at length upon his art; but if there is any truth in a view I offered earlier that one in every three persons is a literary aspirant, with some notion of writing a novel one day, then it would seem that there is an almost limitless and ever-unwearying audience for this sort of reverie. Let us then wander for a while where the Muses haunt. And so celebrate a peace.

I do not think one can arrive at more than some large general ideas about an immensely difficult craft, and about the methods that make for beauty in a novel. The ultimate quality that exalts a novel into the company of the great is probably too elusive for capture and definition. Marlowe has his words for this.

> What is beauty saith my sufferings then?
> If all the pens that ever poets held,
> Had fed the feeling of their masters' thoughts,
> And every sweetness that inspired their hearts,
> Their minds, and muses on admired themes;
> If all the heavenly quintessence they still
> From their immortal flowers of Poesy,
> Wherein as in a mirror we perceive
> The highest reaches of a human wit,
> If these had made one poem's period
> And all combined in beauty's worthiness,
> Yet should there hover in their restless heads,
> One thought, one grace, one wonder at the least,
> Which into words no virtue can digest.

Only a few general ideas then.

Basic to any kind of writing is the handling of our language—though what follows now cannot apply to the novel deliberately and justly written in the tough argot or typical slang of a central tale-teller; it applies only to those novels where the author has to leave the loose slangy dialogue of his characters and write his own descriptions, handling our lovely language well.

How does one know that one handles it well? We all think we do and that it is the other fellow who doesn't, but let us be humble; how can we be really sure that our ear, or our palate, for this richly furnished language is true? All too many people quite plainly suppose that the longer, rounder and more resonant the words, the better their writing. But this won't do at all. It may be true sometimes, or often, of writing that is purely expository, for the weighty and blade-sharp words derived from the classical languages have an exquisite precision. But exposition is only one kind of writing. Roughly there are three kinds, the expository which is addressed to the intellect, the hortatory from pulpit or platform, and the narrative, both of which latter are preponderantly addressed to the emotions—whether they are emotions of pity, humour, alarm, anger, suspense, or what-not—and no abstract polysyllables will evoke a stir of emotion; they are too heavy; they can render a meaning to the intellect perfectly; but they are soporific rather than stimulants. For the stirring of emotion words have to be simple, brief, homely and unpretentious. And concrete rather than abstract. That is why the old advice, 'Anglo-Saxon words for emotion, and the smaller the better' is a good guide; or perhaps we might put it, 'Anglo-Saxon words for the heart; classical words for the brain.' This is not to say that a master of language will not sometimes, deliberately, introduce a long classical word among the humble sort to achieve an ever-memorable effect, as Wordsworth in *The Affliction of Margaret*, mourning her son:

> Or (thou) hast been summoned to the deep,
> Thou, thou and all thy mates, to keep
> An incommunicable sleep.

I sometimes think that if you would learn to write a fine and true English prose you must serve your apprenticeship to poetry. By this I do not mean that you must write poetry, though it will do you no harm to essay some occasional verse (as I know you all have); nor do I mean that you should dress your prose in decorative uniforms which belong only to poetry; I mean that you should have sat at the feet of our finest poets, because poetry is a great school of literary taste. Why do I think this? Simply because the poet is subject to a discipline over which, or by means of which, he must triumph or perish, where as the prose-writer—essayist, novelist, biographer, historian—is less completely subject to this discipline; he may triumph by other means than the quality of his language—by the interest of his subject matter, for example. There have been some magnificent novels written in revolting English. One that leaps to mind is Dreiser's *An American Tragedy*.

(Having written the above paragraph, I see that it can apply only to traditional poetry that flourished in the days before *vers libre*, and before poetry moved into the harsher and rougher areas where it is adventuring now—and where I have been unable, with any confidence, to follow it.)

Here then are two essential qualities which the traditional poet, unlike the prose-writer, had to achieve or fail. First, of course, word perfection—*le mot juste*—the one and only word that will clothe his meaning—no, perhaps not 'clothe' because clothes can be separated from the body—the one and only word that *is* his meaning. Take a small example, Tennyson's 'The Eagle'. Whatever else you care to say about Tennyson, he was certainly a word-master. Consider all the words here; their smallness, their precision, their emotive power. Monosyllables or disyllables all, except for one which is splendidly heavy in the last line.

> He clasps the crag with crooked hands
> Close to the sun in lonely lands. . . .
>
> The wrinkled sea beneath him crawls,
> He watches from his mountain walls,
> And like a thunderbolt he falls.

Of course every conscientious prose-writer strives to achieve this perfection of phrase, but my point remains that it isn't so absolutely essential to him.

The second essential quality: compression. An intense compression. Here the poet brings us to a real heart of the matter, for just in so far as your words are too many, too large, too beautiful for the emotion they express, so far will you be writing inflated or 'purple' stuff; and, conversely, just in so far as your emotion packs out your words, charges them to the utmost, *overcharges* them, perhaps, so that strange, half-hidden, haunting significances escape away into overtones, so far will you be achieving or trembling near to beauty. I could provide a thousand examples of intense compression, but perhaps it will be enough to refer to one recent master of it, A. E. Housman. Never mind how sadly restricted his subject matter may be; just take any poem in his *Shropshire Lad* and you will know all about compression. Monosyllables, monosyllables, so that, if there is a polysyllable its power is heightened.

> Now and I muse for why, and never find the reason;
> I pace the earth, and drink the air, and feel the sun.
> Be still, be still, my soul; it is but for a season;
> Let us endure an hour and see injustice done.

Or, from his *Last Poems*,

The troubles of our proud and angry dust
Are from eternity and shall not fail.
Bear them we can, and if we can we must.
Shoulder the sky, my lad, and drink your ale.

A single verse is just ringing in my heart to be included, ringing as it does with the smallest of small words.

Sing me a song of a lad that is gone;
Say, could that lad be I?
Merry of soul he sailed on a day
Over the sea to Skye.

Or its yet more famous variant:

Hail, bonny boat, like a bird on the wing,
Homeward, the sailors cry,
Carry the lad that's born to be king
Over the sea to Skye.

For the half-hidden and haunting overtones take a few sentences from Shakespeare (though he, even he, could err often and over-inflate his verse).

Macduff and Malcolm are in England; Ross comes to Macduff to break to him the awful news that Macbeth, up in Scotland, has surprised his castle, slain Lady Macduff and all his children. Here are some of the sentences; I will leave them with little comment. Note only the monosyllables.

Macduff: How does my wife?
Ross: Why, well.
Macduff: And all my children?
Ross: Well too.
Macduff: They tyrant has not battered at their peace?
Ross: No; they were well at peace when I did leave them.
Macduff: Be not a niggard of your speech. How goes it?

And Ross tells all.

Malcolm (to Macduff): What, man! Ne'er pull your hat upon your
brows; give sorrow words; the grief that does not speak whispers
the o'er-fraught heart and bids it break.

Macduff: My children too?

Ross: Wife, children, servants, all that could be found.

Macduff: And I must be from thence! My wife killed too?

Ross: I have said.

Malcolm: Be comforted. Let's make us medicines of our great
revenge to cure this deadly grief.

Macduff: He has no children. All my pretty ones? Did you say all?
All? What, all my pretty chickens and their dam at one fell
swoop?

Malcolm: Dispute it like a man.

Macduff: I shall do so. But I must also feel it as a man.

In that last monosyllabic sentence, do not overtones escape away,
so that it is charged, not only with Macduff's tragedy in this hour,
but with something of the tragedy of all our human kind?

§

Throughout my years of writing I have had a suspicion that many
modern critics, and probably the majority of them, are badly astray
in their evaluation of current fiction, and that, consequently, the last
fifty years have been inimical to the creation of great fiction—or of
what seems great fiction to me. In other words, only those novelists
who have written against the tide of criticism have created novels
which, being independent of their day and date, will win the favour
of posterity. I once delivered myself of this tentative view in a lecture
at Leeds University entitled 'A Novelist Reviews the Reviewers'. I'd
had a fancy to call it 'The Worm Turns', but decided that this was
too frivolous a title for such academic surroundings. In it I submitted
—with humility as I hoped—that much contemporary criticism might
be mistaken but, greatly to my surprise, for I felt quite innocent, my
lecture was savagely attacked next morning in a *Yorkshire Post* leader
as an arrogant performance and 'the usual spectacle of an embittered
author infuriated by hostile criticism which he didn't expect and
didn't think he deserved'.

Well . . . well . . . one gets weary at times of this assumption that if an author criticizes the criticism of his day it can only be because he is incensed by the critical treatment meted out to him. It is at least possible that he is merely as interested as any other person in the intellectual climate of his day and its influence on contemporary literature. I was given to understand that this angry article was written by one of the paper's principal critics; if so, it certainly suggested that critics themselves are often among those who cannot take criticism. However, perhaps the fault was mine in that I phrased my tentative thesis badly.

The substance of the lecture—and I still think it had some truth in it—was this: that the excessive sentimentality of so many nineteenth-century writers, their too comfortable idealism, their too easy optimism —these things, followed by the shattering disenchantment of the First World War, had produced a reaction that was itself excessive and sentimental, if by 'sentimentality' we meant an emotionally driven recoil from reality. I said, 'We are now frightened of sufficiently expressed emotion; this, I feel, is a fatal phobia in our time. And I'm not speaking now of critics only but of us all; of you; of me. All of us here, unless we have been able to escape the pressure of the time have (I am submitting) been over-conditioned to recoil with distaste from any full and fearless expression of the tenderer emotions, and any full and fearless treatment of the sweetness in life, such as it is. I want you next time you recoil from something too "sweet", too "sentimental", to ask yourself, Is it just possible that this response of mine which *seems* so right, so true, is in fact untrustworthy? Untrustworthy because it is an over-conditioned reflex. You may be right; you probably *are* right, but I want you to be not too sure. If these are over-conditioned reflexes, how can the greatest literature thrive in an atmosphere so frightened and so cold?'

What is it that is absolute, eternal, undated, in the greatest literature? I sweep the literature of my own country and so far as I can (which is not far) the literature of other lands, and always the answer comes to me that this absolute thing, independent of any age, climate, or passing fashion, is the fearless and therefore sufficient (but not excessive) expression of the natural human emotions. And that is why I often fear that our present shivering away from adequately expressed 'sentimental' and heroic emotions—unless we rise superior to it—can issue only in an arid, constricted, and constipated literature. And, further, that this distaste for any strong expression of emotion is a completely transient thing.

In the lecture I continued—and it was probably this that earned me the caning from the *Yorkshire Post* critic: 'I would like to see a powerful movement of writers who entirely refuse to obey this present time-spirit, preferring to stand apart from it, let the critics savage them as they like. If the critics are the reflection of the waves about them, then such writers would recognize these for dangerous waves, and brief and passing waves, and beat up against them, setting their course, not by the currents about them, but by the stationary stars above. So far from trying to produce work that reflects their time and is to that extent "dated", they would remember that what is "dated" is almost by definition not eternal, and they would turn their eyes away from the demands of current criticism and try to discover what is *absolute* in literary achievement.'

In the greatest works of any age or country, can you see this fear of emotion, this nervous distaste for the describing of it?

Some samples at random.

The Bible. 'And Joseph lifted up his eyes and saw his brother, Benjamin, his mother's son, and said, "Is this your younger brother of whom ye spake unto me?" And he said, "God be gracious unto thee, my son." And Joseph made haste, for his bowels did yearn upon his brother, and he sought where to weep, and he entered into his chamber and wept there.'

'And the king said unto Cushi, "Is the young man, Absalom, safe?" And Cushi answered, "The enemies of my lord the king, and all that rise against thee to do thee hurt, be as that young man is." And the king was much moved, and went up to the chamber over the gate and wept; and as he went, thus he said, "Oh my son, Absalom, my son, my son Absalom. Would God I had died for thee, O Absalom my son, my son."'

From its *Song of Songs*: 'How beautiful are thy feet with shoes, O prince's daughter; the joints of thy thighs are like jewels, the work of the hands of a cunning workman. Thy navel is like a round goblet which wanteth not liquor; thy belly is like a heap of wheat set about with lilies. Thy two breasts are like two young roes that are twins. . . . How fair and how pleasant art thou, O love, for delights.'

The Greeks, whose motto was 'Nothing too much' but never, so far as I know, 'Not enough'. Homer: 'So saying, he sat down, and Tele-

machus, flinging his arms about his father, wept and shed tears; and in
the hearts of both arose a longing for crying. And they wailed aloud
more vehemently than birds . . . sea-eagles . . . whose young the
country-folk have taken from their nest; even so piteously did they
let their tears fall from beneath their brows.'

Euripides: Orestes and Electra, covered with blood, emerge upon
the stage after looking down upon the body of their mother, Clytem-
nestra, whom they have murdered.

> *Electra:* Let tear rain upon tear,
> Brother, but mine is the blame. . . .
> I was the child at her knee
> Mother, I named her name.
> *Orestes:* Sawest thou her raiment there,
> Sister there in the blood?
> She drew it back as she stood,
> She opened her bosom bare,
> She bent her knees to the earth . . .
> And I . . . oh, her hair, her hair. . . .

Shakespeare. In the greatest of his plays, is he afraid?

> Now cracks a noble heart. Goodnight, sweet prince,
> And flights of angels sing thee to thy rest.

Goethe. Gretchen speaking in the condemned cell to Faust:

> I'll tell thee how the graves shall be.
> They'll be thy care tomorrow.
> My mother in the best place lay,
> And close beside her my brother, I pray.
> Me a little space aside,
> But not too wide,
> And my little one lay on my right breast.
> None but my babe by me shall rest.

You may argue that much of this is poetry, where a stronger emotional utterance is tolerable than in prose, but it is still difficult to

think of any modern writer being suffered to give his characters words like these.

Two samples then from undoubted prose.

Chekhov. The closing speech in *Uncle Vanya*, Sonya speaking: 'We shall rest. We shall hear the angels; we shall see all Heaven lit with radiance; we shall see all earthly evil, all our sufferings drowned in mercy which will fill the whole world, and our life will be peaceful, gentle, and sweet as a caress. I have faith, I have faith. (*She wipes away his tears with her handkerchief*) Poor Uncle Vanya, you are crying. You have had no joy in your life, but wait, Uncle Vanya, wait. We shall rest. We shall rest.'

George Eliot. Closing words of *The Mill on the Floss*: 'The boat reappeared, but brother and sister had gone down in an embrace never to be parted, living through again in one supreme moment the days when they had clasped their little hands in love and roamed the daisied fields together.'

Modern criticism has long canonized Chekhov, and lately beatified George Eliot, but I submit that it accepts such shameless expression of the tenderer and sweeter sentiments from these writers only because they have the decency to be dead.

I closed the lecture with some words from Christopher Fry, who cannot phrase other than beautifully. 'Most of us authors are ready to mend our ways, and even eager to mend them, because we love our art, but we cannot trust the critic to tell us how to do so unless he also knows moments of prayer and fasting and self-distrust; unless we can be sure that he gets no pleasure from wounding or from belittling others to give himself the appearance of size.'

But this quotation—humble enough, for goodness sake—did not save me from the virulent attack in the morning and its accusation of arrogance.

§

Most novelists are surprised, in secret, at the wounding way in which some of their friends, normally good men and kind, will speak to them about their novels. This is not to say that familiar friends must never express a less than favourable estimate of one's new book or of an old one; it is the curious, impercipient *hardness* of their words which sometimes surprises one. They have failed to perceive that there is a parental relationship, almost an umbilical relationship, between a novelist and his creation, to which he has given his heart's blood over months or years. One would think that, remembering this, they would give you their criticism, but in gentle words to ease the parental heart. But not so; not so with a few of them; one can even suspect in these few an unconscious satisfaction in doing the opposite. Once a good friend of mine, a clever business man, said to me over a dinner-table in his club, 'I read your books, as you know, but, to be frank, I don't think you've written a good book since *The Marsh*.' He said it with some verve, while I thought, 'Who would say to a parent, "I know your six children well, but I don't think you've produced a nice one since Monica"?' A little stunned by this blunt instrument, I replied (over the sweet), 'Well, I find that comment of some commercial interest because it may reveal what the common-or-garden novel-reader is thinking, but, aesthetically, it doesn't trouble me at all because, to be frank, I don't think you're qualified to judge.' Hotly he retorted, 'Well, I think that's the most conceited remark I've ever heard.' I replied, 'Please, why should it be right and proper for you to disparage my books but shockingly conceited of me to disparage your criticism?'

A pleasant woman, with whom I'd shared a mutual affection over many years, said to me once, when not in her best mood, 'I've just finished your *Morris in the Dance*, and, to be honest, I really can't think why publishers trouble to publish such books.'

No less than this did she say.

Now, as a matter of fact, I, too, think this book an unsatisfactory work, but my business here is to inquire, 'What good friend would say to a novelist who has fathered boys and girls, "I really can't think why your wife troubles to produce for you children like your Alexander?"'

Doubtless Alexander is imperfect, but sympathizers would express their sense of this in gentler terms. Certainly, if he is a child. Far less assuredly, if he is a novel.

§

Fortunately, to compensate for these sabre-thrusts, a novelist gets his flatteries. He gets his 'fan mail', some of it fully intelligent, some less so, some a shade ridiculous, but all and any of it, I'm afraid, equally pleasing. The oddest (but still pleasing) 'fan letter' I ever received came from Nigeria, and the sender's name on the back of the aerogramme was 'Young Sunday Ojo'. It ran: 'Dear friend, how happy I am to get your delighted address in Daily Mirro, and how happy I am I will be sending you some carving wood when I get your reply. I want to have you as my pen pal in Oversea. I am 16 years old with handsome face and stand 5 ft. 6 ins. tall. I have just posted my photo to you through Over Sea Mail. I am yours faithfully Young Sunday Ojo.'

This letter reminds me of one which, perhaps, was not so totally pleasing. It came from some unknown girl-reader and contained the sentence: 'Yours is my ideal face. Not over-handsome, but full of character.' Some satisfying pieces of flattery are spoken, not written. Once I was lecturing to a Literary Society in Cork on 'The Craft of the Novel'. Cork, you may remember, is only a mile or so from Blarney Castle. The lecture seemed to be faring reasonably well, but not to be achieving, in any high degree, 'an outstanding success'. Nevertheless an elderly Irishwoman came rushing up to me to say in her lovely southern brogue, 'Oh, Mr Raymond, it was not the lecture of the season; it was the lecture of the ages.'

Thanking her, I submitted that she could hardly have said more. Demosthenes was nowhere. Nor Cicero. Nor any other of history's great orators. And I assured her I would go out and kiss that Blarney Stone tomorrow.

Which I did.

Perhaps I was consoled for that 'not over-handsome face' one day when I was having my photograph taken by Messrs Elliot and Fry. The photographer in their studio, a simple, kindly, encouraging old gentleman, said, 'You are an author, I understand?'

I agreed, and he proceeded, 'Well now, don't worry about me. Just forget I'm here. Just sit there and think your wonderful thoughts.'

I did as I was bidden. I sat there and tried to think wonderful thoughts; and I must say that the photograph the old gentleman took was quite most satisfying—and flattering—I have ever had done. For as long as I honestly could—and for longer—I used it when invited by some journal to send a photograph 'for publicity purposes'.

On another occasion I had just returned from Sweden, and was wearing a newly bought grey suit. I am very tall but it is easy to get ready-made suits for the very tall in that country largely composed of giants. Anyhow the suit was finely broad-shouldered and of palpable Scandinavian rather than English cut. And as I wore it, walking towards my Hampstead home, one from a group of loathsome little boys called out to his mates as he gaped at me, 'Oh, look at that super-spiv.' It is always pleasant to be super.

§

Let us muse on those things which make for success in a novel, whether popular success, critical success, or both; and conversely those which lay on it a cold hand of death.

One thing generally lethal to popular success, however good parts of the story may be, is when the central character 'plays against the house'; when he stirs in his audience, not sympathy, but dislike. (There are exceptions to this rule—*Hatter's Castle* occurs to me—but they are rare. It needn't apply in the least to the critical reception of the novel.) One novel of mine brought this truth romping home to me. Called *The Chatelaine*, it was a study of a woman whose affection overflowed like a flooding river, but in words only; it could not induce her to sacrifice herself for anybody, even her son. (Readers of my first volume may guess what inspired this idea.) She has a villa in France which she calls her 'chateau'; her son's aeroplane, in the Second War, crashes behind the enemy lines; evading the enemy he seeks her door in the night, but she sends him away—with loving words—that her beloved little 'chateau' may not be endangered, and he has to wander away and hide himself in a forest. She never forgives herself for this; repents bitterly; seeks to make amends, and is forgiven by the son—but not by my readers. Whatever her remorse, they could not take that turning of her son adrift into the perilous night; and the book, after a falling sale, found its way into the Remainder market.

Oddly, one can set against this my *We, the Accused*, which, though it studies a murderer from his first conception of the crime to his fall through the scaffold-drop, has been a steady seller for thirty years and is indeed my second most popular novel. How is this? Plainly, I fear, because readers dislike his wife far more than they dislike him, and they are, if not delighted, comfortably satisfied to see her murdered;

they are ready, alas, to 'harbour and assist him'. And in the closing scene he pays the full and dreadful penalty with some courage. So I suppose that, really, he didn't play against the house.

A better illustration, perhaps, since I may see my own books too indulgently, is a fine novel of my wife's, *Guest of Honour*, in which, truthfully and fearlessly, she shows her central character committing an outrageous act. The book won the suffrages of the critics but not the popular success it deserved. I would regard it as the 'second best' of my wife's novels. It has not the total unity of mood or the perfect close of a later novel, *People in the House*; which for me, as I always say (though I may be partial, but others have agreed with me), is at least a candidate queueing before the crowded turnstiles that lead towards posterity.

A second thing that either 'makes' a novel or maims it is enshrined in the words, *Finis coronat opus*, 'the end crowns the work', which carries as its corollary, 'the end can uncrown and depose the work'. This was fully demonstrated to me only lately in a book called *One of Our Brethren*. This novel was based on a celebrated case where an archdeacon was accused of immorality and convicted, though, to this day, there are people who wonder if he was really guilty. I brought the story to a climax which, I imagined, crowned it perfectly, the arch-deacon on his death-bed receiving the Sacrament of Penance, which must have involved a confession of guilt, if guilty he was. *But*—it is an inviolable law of the Church that anything confessed to a priest in this sacrament is *sub sigillo*—under the seal of the confessional for ever. Well pleased with this close I wrote proudly of the ministering priest, 'Now he knew. He alone in all the world. And he alone in all the world would ever know. For him only *Veritas temporis filia*, Truth was the daughter of Time.' I am still sure this close was right aesthetic-ally; but it was wrong commercially; it didn't 'crown the work' for the great majority. People don't want to shut a book in any doubt. Reader after reader complained to me that he or she didn't know the answer to the query running through the book and had laid it aside disappointed—though I should have thought that, whatever the archdeacon confessed on his death-bed, the truth was being partly, if slowly, unveiled all through the later chapters. But—*sub sigillo*; I wasn't going to cry it aloud.

Another thing all important for a novel's *perfect* success, both popu-lar and critical, is that its chief character should sit firmly in the middle of the book. *David Copperfield* is probably the most popular novel in our language, and so great are its treasures that it triumphs over any artistic failure, but artistically it is spoiled by the fact that David, the protagonist, though charming as a boy, is knocked almost out of sight by Mr Micawber, Mrs Micawber, the Peggotys, Barkis (who was willing), Betsy Trotwood and other glorious 'supporting' characters. No one questions that Proust's *A la Recherche du Temps Perdu* is one of the century's great novels, but here again it falls short of perfection because the chief character, Marcel, though he is a wonderful perceiving instrument, reading like a microscope the deepest deeps of the many characters that thrash about in the book, remains himself less a creature of flesh and blood than they, and gets shouldered by them to the sides of the stage. Charlus, Swann, Odette, Albertine, the Duchesse de Guermantes have the flesh and the blood—prick them, and they would bleed. But would he?

The older classical novels often fail in this respect because they were little interested in pure artistic 'form', but here are a few in which the chief character holds splendidly the middle of the stage, no character more dominant than he or she: *Anna Karenina, Madame Bovary, The Mill on the Floss, Far from the Madding Crowd, Crime and Punishment, Lord Jim*. Often two characters of equal value are the principals, playing opposite each other in a *pas de deux*—is it significant that these paired lovers first jump into mind from novels by women?—but surely Jane and Mr Rochester, Catherine Earnshaw and Heathcliff should be mentioned in despatches here.

What, for me, are some of the criteria wherewith to measure 'greatness' in a novel?

First comes the great gushing creative fount which throws up magnificent characters for our delight or our taut interest—Fielding, Smollett, Scott, Dickens, Tolstoy, Dostoievsky, Proust, and even some of our writers still alive.

Second, a narrative skill which leads the reader onward with an elastic leash which may stretch but must never snap. This demands, for me, a plot interest, but the plot must never seem contrived, only inevitable.

Third, a depth of insight into the complexities and inconsistences of every truly human character—Tolstoy and Proust being unsurpassed exemplars of this.

Fourth, a masterly handling of words, often with a beauty as of poetry, when the novelist is not writing dialogue but speaking with his own voice.

And fifth, last, and most important of all, the novelist's philosophy of Life, his vision of Reality, which lies behind all his story, determines his selection of incident, conflict, and drama, and gives 'significance' to his novel.

This philosophy, or criticism of life, must never be explicit. Let it be explicit, a warm argument, perhaps, and the novel has turned into a tract, a pamphlet, a device for propaganda; and this is death. The writer's vision of Reality must lie around his story, or fall from it, as an unspoken but inevitable by-product.

In an autobiography, however, a novelist can and perhaps should be explicit, so may I close this musing chapter with a statement of the 'Vision of Things' which, I hope, inspires my fiction and falls from it like a by-product. It can best be defined as the *applied* Christianity' to which I referred in my first volume. I wrote there, 'I have never, since I have been capable of proper reasoning, doubted that the Christian ethic, *applied* Christianity as distinct from dogmatic Christianity, is the whole truth and the only way of raising humans to their noblest potential.' I would like now to enlarge upon this 'applied Christianity'. Heavy words and cold, both of them, like those I mentioned above, and therefore unevocative, unlikely to stir the emotional deeps, but the one true, perfect Anglo-Saxon monosyllabic word that should touch the deeps has become so devalued and worn as to have lost all immediate potency; it is, of course, 'love'. Loving one's neighbour as oneself; love that grows strong and sane enough to overthrow the natural man's vindictiveness and to realize at last (as I wanted to say to the sergeant when he was preaching 'frightfulness' against the Nazis) that you can never overcome evil by itself in the form of violent vengeance though one's natural blood seems to scream for it; that in brief, violence can never produce anything but itself, and 'love is the only thing that *works*'—which last words, I fancy, would have left the good sergeant still more confused than he was at the time.

Does this mean that a fully practising Christian must be a pacifist? Not necessarily, if we are using this word to describe a political belief as to what a *nation* should do. I have never been able to see how a nation of, say, 50,000,000 people, all differing in spiritual and intellectual values and stature, can move as a single pacifist unit. But the individual can. In personal relationships he can be a hundred-per-cent pacifist, abjuring, against his natural inclinations, all vengeance, all blows for blows, eyes for eyes, evil for evil. It is difficult. As Bossuet, Bishop of Meaux and great Christian orator, summed it up: 'There is no wider difference in the world than between living according to nature and living according to grace.'

But, you may be warming up to ask, where stands the novel in all this rarefied ethical air, the novel which is an artefact designed to entertain, divert, and give aesthetic pleasure, not moral exhortation? Well, certainly a novelist's business is to delight us with his story, his comedy, his drama, his pathos, and with the beauty of his book's formal shape; certainly, as we agreed above, the moment a novel begins to preach, it degenerates into a tract and steps into its coffin; *but*—and this is a very big 'but', properly italicized—*but*, granted that the writing of a novel must be driven and controlled by purely aesthetic considerations; granted that it should be written less out of one's discursive reason than out of one's emotions and imaginations and intuitive perceptions, the reason acting only as a mechanical 'governor' to prevent the emotions from running amok; granted all this: there still remains, inevitably, this by-product or fall-out from any novel, and my contention here is that, in nearly all the greatest novels, it is almost bound to be a Christian by-product, a Christian fall-out.

This is going to take some proving. A novel contains what? Characters, plot, significant drama, and this unspoken philosophy or spiritual vision of the author. A novelist, or any artist in any medium, is what? Ideally—though no man is a pure artist; usually he is an amalgam of artist, salesman, and self-regarder—but, ideally, an artist is not just an entertainer, he is, or should be, a being more highly sensitive to, more responsive to, more profoundly stirred, troubled, and quickened by the pageant, the magic, the mystery and the wonder of the world; by the comedy, the tragedy, the stupidity and the heroism of his human kind; and, by some strange ordinance of nature, he is so made that he can know neither healing nor peace till he has got this emotion raised within him into some form that, for *him*, is beautiful. Why this should be the psychological need of the artist who can say? But there it is.

And now I want to suggest that this high response to the comedy, tragedy, follies, gaiety and braveries of mankind must nearly always drive the novelist's creations, his art-forms, in the direction of pity.

I suggest that fiction becomes great when it creates, not primarily exciting incidents (though, perhaps, the more of these the merrier) but exciting interpretations; when it seeks to reveal, not so much what people did as why they did it; and this—to be less interested in what a person has done than why he has done it—is the beginning of charity. Wherefore I shall dare to say that great literature, or that part of it which is great fiction, is a service to the community because it can bring us to charity, vision, and the tragic pity which helps to make men great.

I like to call the novelist a 'professional imaginer', by which I mean that his task is to *imagine much further* than most hard-worked men and women have time to do; and then to incarnate these deeper imaginings into a story that will enthral a reader and raise in him a deep understanding of the characters, with laughter for their follies and tears for their tragedies—and if you will look at these three things, insight, laughter, and tears, you will see that they are the very symptoms of generous pity. The novelist must carry his reader's tired or sluggish imagination all the way that his own imagination has travelled; he should make his reader suddenly aware, with some dismay, of the shallows in his own imagination. Many people, perhaps the majority, have imaginations so restricted that they cannot see without their eyes. They are instant in condemnation and in demand for painful punishment—until they see the sinner and his whole environment with their eyes. Often in war I have heard simple British soldiers, infuriated by atrocities alleged of Germans, avow (like my sergeant) 'Jerry's getting no mercy from me', and yet, when they got a weary, worn-out, bewildered German prisoner in their hands, it was, "Ere, Fritzy, have a fag.' They were seeing at last with their eyes. It is noteworthy that, in '14-'18, this manner of 'tough' talk by British soldiers was heard mainly in the first year of war, rarely in the later years; by then they had lived to see with their eyes. Similarly it is often told of prison officers that they may speak ruthless words about some notorious murderer, but when they have got him in the condemned cell, none so ready to show him mercy. This may not apply if the man is visibly a brutal thug, but ninety per cent of murderers are something much less than this, and when their jailers have them in their keeping, they see them with their eyes.

Let us list some novels that bear out my contention. What is Flaubert's *Madame Bovary* but the story of a foolish and typical little woman 'taken in adultery'? When Flaubert was standing outside his novel, he said, '*Madame Bovary, c'est moi*'; and to George Sand he declared plainly, 'I don't want condemnation and anger but only sympathy; and of this one cannot have enough.'

Dickens was often ready to turn his novel for a moment into a tract. Remember again the death of Poor Joe, which I quoted in my earlier volume: 'Dead, your Majesty. Dead, my lords and gentlemen. Dead, Right Reverends and Wrong Reverends of every order. Dead, men and women born with heavenly compassion in your hearts. And dying thus around us every day.'

Wells was always capable of an equal naughtiness; he would glory, 'I'm not an artist; I'm a journalist.' And in *Mr Polly* he really sets about being explicit. Leaving Mr Polly, he turned to 'a certain dome-headed sociologist' who, in his opinion was handling in a 'bloodless, dry-as-dust, inhuman unhelpful manner' his social problems, and he dealt with him faithfully. 'There on the one hand is the man of under-standing who sees clearly the big process that dooms millions of lives to thwarting and discomfort and unhappy circumstances, but giving us no help, no hint, by which we could dam that stream of human failure; and there, on the other hand, is Mr Polly sitting on his gate, untrained, unwarned, confused, distressed, angry, seeing nothing except that he is, as it were, netted in greyness and discomfort—with all life dancing about him—Mr Polly with a capacity for joy and beauty at least as keen and subtle as yours and mine.'

(This from an atheist who scoffed at Christianity.)

Dostoievsky—every one of his novels is almost a tormented cry for a Christly pity. Tolstoy in his *What is Art?*, oddly aberrant as he may be about the canons of art, yet makes my point for me by proclaiming that Art must be religious in origin and should convey its religious message to the great masses of men. So too Goethe: 'Art rests upon a religious sense because of its deep immutable earnestness. That is why Art so readily identifies itself with religion.' So Arnold Bennett, the thrusting hedonist: 'The essential characteristic of the really great novelist is a Christ-like all-embracing compassion.' A quiet comment by Chekhov on his works: 'One must forgive. It would be strange not to forgive.' Blake was not a novelist but he asserted that the creative imagination was for him 'the Christ' and that 'All serious art is the sister of religion'. D. H. Lawrence, writing to a correspondent about the pains of artistic creation, says, 'I always feel as if I stood naked for the fire of Almighty God to go through me. One has to be terribly religious to be an artist.' And again elsewhere: 'Primarily I am a passionately religious man, and my novels must be written from the depths of my religious experience.' So recent and 'modern' an influence as Eugène Ionesco, in his *Journal*: 'I have always tried to believe in God. Not naïve, not subtle enough. But I have not completely burned all my bridges with God. . . . How difficult it is to forgive our enemies. How can we avoid hating them? Nevertheless, vengeance gives neither satisfaction nor compensation; what's the good of it once the wrong has been done?' John Cowper Powys in his *Pleasures of Literature*: 'This is still, and ever will be, the "over-soul" in all books . . . the burden from the beginning until this hour has been the same—by Justice, by Tolerance, and by Pity is the real Evolution known.' Which he stresses again in his last words: 'It may well be that what gives us the deepest happiness we know is merely to touch (in books) that level, that dimension, that plane of existence, from which proceeds the inexplicable imperative to follow goodness and mercy in a world built upon a different plan.'

What I find comforting in all this is the apparent fact that all men, if only they will imagine deep enough, tend to arrive at the same vision. It is a commonplace that all mystics of whatever race or religion say the same thing in the end about love and forgiveness and the futility, as well as the wrongness, of vengeance; and here we have these lesser men, the novelists, sinners not saints, but all arriving at the same vision—which happens to be applied Christianity.

II

1

INTO THE FIFTIES AND SIXTIES

It is the year '68, as I write, twenty-four years after the Home Guard stood down and the Second War drew to its close; and it is pleasant—perhaps exceptional—to record that in each of those twenty-four years, nearly a quarter of a century, there has been in Hampstead, round about Christmas, a reunion of those who were Home Guards together in the fading past. In the first ten of these years the reunion was a Christmas feast with turkey and plum pudding, and early in the course of these annual feasts, an extraordinary ritual established itself for performance, when dinner was over, coffee on the table, and pipes lit. I have told how, after two years as a private in the Hampstead Home Guard I reached the rank of lance-corporal. Another who achieved no less was Private Malcolm Thomson, now a parson, but then a civil servant who was also an author, having written among other books a monumental life of Lloyd George. The new ritual determined that it was only decent, indeed incumbent, on two authors in this Old H.G. Club to write a poem for the annual reunion and for each to rise in his place and read the offering of his fellow lance-corporal. Here is some of Malcolm's poem for our tenth anniversary celebration. It must be explained that 'Fuerst', then head of Fuerst Bros., a big firm of Colonial and Overseas Produce Merchants, was our cook when we went into camp. Therefore he was the natural organizer of our 'feasts' in the Holmefield Court Restaurant in Hampstead, and the generous provider of the turkey.

> A sombre silence swathed the Heath.
>> No sparrow chirped. No pigeon coo'ed.
> No fox nor badger barked beneath
>> The laurel coverts of Ken Wood.
> In Hampstead ponds no frigid frog
>> Croaked out a curse upon the smog.
>
> The rain dripped silent on the shrubs.
>> In Willow Road the willows wept.
> The pots lay empty in the pubs.
>> Behind their bars the potmen slept
> When sudden from the silence burst
>> A frenzied cook-house call from Fuerst.

'Turn out, ye toughs of A Platoon,
　　Home Guards of Hampstead hear my howl!
The board at Holmefield Court is strewn
　　With wallop jugs and Christmas fowl!
In bygone days ye trained for fights.
　　Now prove you've trained your appetites.

'Nine times in former years at least
　　Your ranks have rallied to the board.
This is your tenth high Home Guard feast!
　　Come, lusty warriors, in a horde.
Rheumatics, gout, and age defy.
　　Prove that old soldiers never die.'

(Silence descends upon the Heath,
　　But through the silence comes
Clatter of worn and artificial teeth
　　　And mumbling gums.)

And here is one verse from the other lance-corporal's poem. You
will remember that our Headquarters had been in the evacuated Queen
Mary's Maternity Home.

Oh, where are the boys of the old Platoon?
God bless them, I fancy that, ghostly and grey,
Their figures are seen by the light of the moon
On Heath, at street corners, or over the way
(Each creeping along with bayonet fixed,
Most anxious to please but a trifle perplexed,
For new orders have come and the O.C. is vexed,
And no one on earth can interpret the text);
I surmise that the boys of the old Platoon
Thus haunt their old hills by the light of the moon,
And surely at midnight their grey phantoms roam
Through the rooms and the wards of the Maternity Home.

But all this was in the first years when the attendances were good,
but now—well now we are but few and we just sit around and drink
beer together in the Freemasons' Arms. Generally we are but nine or

ten and when our secretary, ex-Home Guard Sergeant Russell who, like all honorary secretaries alone holds our little and dwindling company together, has read the Minutes—minutes, if you please, of the last meeting of nine or ten—he usually adds that, in our name, he has expended a guinea or two on a wreath for one of the old brotherhood who has 'passed on'. Thereafter all is talk, falling sooner or later into memories about the old years of '40 to '44, when we 'remember with advantages' perhaps, what mighty feats we did in that strange heroic time.

§

Three times in the fifties, in '53, '56, and '59, when the triennial elections to the Hampstead Borough Council were held I contested the Town Ward in the Liberal interest, more for the sake of flying the Liberal flag than with any hope of success, and indeed I had no success except that I slightly increased the Liberal vote each time and even carried it into second place in '59. What happened in '62 is quite another matter.

In order to come to it I must first write of a fact that brought much happiness to my wife and myself. Pamela Frankau came to live in Hampstead 'only a few yards round the corner' from us. Pamela was my wife's cousin, but as Diana wrote in an introduction to Pamela's last book, their relationship was something much fuller than that 'barren word', cousin, usually implies. Pamela, some years older, had been the heroine of Diana's childhood and the strongest influence in her life. And now we had her within immediate reach, together with Margaret Webster, the fine actress and famous play-producer, who shared a home with her. Thus all four of us, Pam, Peggy, Diana and myself could sit in my study or their drawing-room and talk for hours on the arts of fiction and play-production; the sins of critics, the deficiencies of publishers, the endless humours of back-stage, the skimping royalties paid to authors as compared with costs or discounts allowed to printers, binders or booksellers, and all the other splendours and miseries of the writing life. Pamela was the wittiest person I have ever known—at least I have never met a wittier. Perhaps our good friend and brilliant novelist, R. C. Hutchinson, is her equal. Anyhow, I remember an evening when Pam and Ray and Margaret Hutchinson came to dinner with us, and after dinner the talk contracted into a duologue between Pam and Ray, with the rest of us more than happy to sit around, saying nothing, and loosing yells of laughter for two hours or more as these two exchanged their stories and wisecracks about life in the army and in the dafter corners of the book world.

Sometimes, visiting one another, we talked politics, and though she was not a member of the Liberal Party, as I was, her attitude to most topical questions approximated always to the Liberal line. So one spring evening, when the Hampstead Borough elections were looming, and I had agreed to fight the Town Ward for the fourth time, hoping to maintain the second position we'd won three years before, I suddenly hastened to my telephone and rang Pamela. I said, 'You'll agree, Pam, that though in the field of arithmetic twice one makes two, it is not necessarily so in other fields of human experience.'

She said, 'I'll willingly agree if that'll make you happy, but I don't know what you're talking about.'

So I explained, 'Well look, if Heinemann's advertise the title of your next book or your name *twice* in a single newspaper panel, in tabular form and heavy type, e.g. PAMELA FRANKAU, PAMELA FRANKAU, the impact is at least three times as great as if they'd only printed it once, and I would even go so far as to suggest in this example twice one is four.'

She agreed that this was extremely probable, and she would promptly draw Heinemann's attention to it, and it was nice of me to be thinking about her books, but what, pray, was all this really leading up to?

'It is leading up to this, dear Pam: that it would be false modesty on my part to deny that I've been helped in my three previous candidatures for the Borough Council by being a novelist with a fairly large readership, and—well—if the Liberals were to field *two* novelists in this new Town Ward poll, twice one might equal three—even four.'

'Yes. And so what?'

'Come, Pam. Be your usual bright self. Will *you* stand? Along with me?'

The idea amused her, and after a minute or two she said, 'I think I'd stand, if you can promise me on your honour that I shan't get in.'

I replied, 'Of that there isn't a hope in hell. You'd be quite safe. In all its history our Tory-controlled council has never had a Liberal, and of all its seven wards the Town Ward is said to be the Tories' strongest citadel. No Liberal ever gets in there.'

'Oh, well . . .' she began.

And I interrupted encouragingly with 'It's really only a matter of keeping the flag flying.'

'Oh, well . . . in that case . . .' she said.

And that was that. I rang our Liberal Headquarters to tell them that Pamela Frankau would stand if invited; and they were overjoyed. We had another strong candidate in the Town Ward, Archie Macdonald, who'd been Liberal M.P. for Roxburgh and Selkirk until 1957, so our campaign started with a flourish; and we hoped to make at least as good a showing as last time; but could hope for little more.

A week or so before the election, which was on May 10th, Pamela rang me up to ask 'How are things going?' and I answered, hesitating, 'Well . . .' not replying to her query, but expressing some doubt and dismay.

'Well, what?'

'Well, I'm sorry, Pam dear—I apologize profusely—but I'm afraid they're going rather well. Unfortunately there's this strong wind blowing from Orpington'—the astounding Liberal victory in a Parliamentary election at Orpington was only just behind us—'and, you see, you see, we have a remarkable team of Young Liberal canvassers under Bob Somper, and they report——'

She interrupted, 'I'll sue you for damages if I get in.'

'Oh, there's no fear of that,' I assured her for her comfort. 'But . . . we are undoubtedly doing well. We're going to make a good show. But . . . "not to worry".'

The election day came—and passed; and next morning the Count took place in the Town Hall. It's a serious and stern business, a Count; nobody can venture near it, except the counting assistants, the candidates and their 'spouses', as the Law phrases it, the Borough Returning Officer and his assistants, and a few other persons who can produce from somewhere a legitimate reason for a special pass. Once you are in the Hall, having passed the vigilantes 'on the door', you are not allowed out. A policeman stands at the door to stop any such exit, and only a very exceptional and powerfully ratified excuse will get you past him.

The Count took hours. Some of us ate sandwiches we had bought, suspecting we wouldn't be able to escape for a meal. Two recounts were claimed in two of the borough's seven wards, and it was nearly three o'clock when the Town Clerk, as Returning Officer, rose to announce a result.

Town Ward: Pamela had topped the poll defeating even the Tories' strongest candidate, Dame Barbara Brooke, wife of Henry Brooke, our Tory member. Archie Macdonald and I were also elected. Three Liberals in the Hampstead Borough Council for the first time in its history. And in its Town Ward. Someone called it 'a little Orpington'.

Liberals had done well in the other six wards but not to the point of getting elected. I still maintain that in some cases twice one equals three, or, if you like, three times one equals four. Or maybe five.

One of our women supporters in the Town Ward, an elderly lady who'd worked all her life for the Liberal Party, came to the Town Hall door when she heard that the results were pinned up there, read that three of the candidates for whom she had laboured were 'in', and there on the steps of the Town Hall stood and wept. She had to go to the National Gallery to quiet the excitement and happiness in her heart.

Pamela had been unable to get to the Count so I rang her up to tell her of her success, to apologize, and to state that I would accept service of a writ on her behalf, unless we could settle out of court. But of course she was delighted by my news. How could she be other than delighted with such a triumph and such a local tribute to her name? And a fine councillor she made, dutiful, hard-working, witty, and greatly popular—until illness in a savage form struck her down. Enjoying the work on committees and in the Council Chamber, she assured me many a time that she wouldn't, for anything, have missed this experience as a borough councillor.

The old Hampstead Borough Council used to stage its monthly council meetings with full ceremony, the whole company of councillors rising when the aldermen entered in their scarlet and furred robes to take their places on the aldermanic bench; and then while all of us remained standing, came the Mayor's Procession: Mace Bearer with golden mace, Town Clerk in wig, gown, and bands, and Mayor in scarlet robes like the aldermen, with golden chain of office, white lace jabot and white gloves.

Pamela's comment on this Solemn Entry, the first time she saw it from her place on the Liberal bench, was 'The bit I like best is when the aldermen all come in dressed as each other.'

Of Pamela Chandler's fine picture of Pamela Frankau facing page

87 I must report that Noel Coward, on first seeing it, said, 'Now that's what I've always wanted to look like but never can.'

§

I would often discuss with Pamela those comic stories which stand high above all others because they enclose something eternally true to all human experience; something quintessential and not just relative or *ad hoc*. Such a one is that of the wife asking her husband, 'Did you notice anything different about me at breakfast this morning?' *Husband:* 'No, darling. What was it?' *Wife:* 'I wasn't there.' I particularly like the husband's perfectly genuine 'darling' in that story. Another, of course, is that of the child looking at the picture of Christian martyrs being devoured by the lions in the Colosseum and complaining, 'Oh, Mummy, one poor lion hasn't got a Christian.' Infinitely true of the small child who is naïvely unaware that the prudish days of its parents have long ago passed is the song-refrain we owe to Michael Flanders and Donald Swann:

> Ma's out, Pa's out,
> Let's talk rude.
> Pee, po, belly, bum, drawers.

H. H. Munro ('Saki') will remain immortal, if for nothing else, for his desperate sentence, 'She was a good cook as cooks go; and as cooks go, she went.' Universally true to parents, at least, is their vivid appreciation of the line in the hymn, 'Peace, perfect peace, with loved ones far away.' Of Shakespearean lines, fluffed by over-tired actors, what comes nearer to universal life than his lovely song varied to 'What is love? 'Tis not her father'; or—if this is not too merely Freudian a fluff—'All the world's a stage and all the men and women merely players; And each man in his time pays many tarts.' True to all wives, or nearly so, is the answer of one at her golden wedding to the question, 'Do you mean to say that you have been married to your husband for fifty years and have never had a thought of divorce?' Her answer: 'Divorce? Good gracious, no! Murder, yes.' Which carries me to a story which it would perhaps be libellous to call characteristic of all Frenchmen. A Frenchman guest at a golden wedding asked, 'What is meant by zis "golden wedding"? I do not understand "golden wedding".'

Informant: 'Why, it simply means that this man and this woman have lived happily together for fifty years.'

Frenchman: 'Oh, I zee. And now zey marry.'

Better than the story of the 'Emperor's Clothes' for expressing the tendency of all to pretend to knowledge they do not possess is that of the Tibetan Eelhound. A man entered his Tibetan Eelhound at Cruft's Dog Show, and since not one of the judges had seen a dog like it before, but did not wish to disclose his ignorance, they gave it a prize. Afterwards one of them asked the owner for more information about this interesting dog, and received the answer, 'Oh, don't you know? They are bred by the monks in Tibet and round up the eels at sunset.'

After which the judge sought his home.

And has anything ever been truer than the weary remark of an Irishman, after queueing an hour outside the gallery door of a theatre: 'Sure it's meself that'd rather walk ten miles than stand five.'

2

COLERIDGE'S TOMB

In '61 there occurred the one event in my life which not only fulfilled a dream to the utmost but transcended it.

My flat is in a block pleasantly standing on the very grass of Hampstead Heath, and often, after a morning at my desk, I have taken my exercise by walking over the Heath's green uplands to the Highgate Ponds and into Highgate Village, forever charming with its eighteenth-century houses, one of which was Coleridge's home in the last years of his life.

A lover of Coleridge, I had, in '53, induced the St Pancras Council to affix a fine plaque to this house, No. 3, The Grove. Unveiled by Sir Harold Nicolson, it showed the words:

> Samuel Taylor Coleridge
> English Poet and Critic
> Lived in Highgate Village for nineteen years
> And in this House
> From 1823 until his death in 1834

But when it was that I found a padlock loose on the gate of a disused churchyard, once the little cemetery around the old Highgate Chapel where Coleridge used to worship; and, entering, walked into a kind of crypt open to the weather where Coleridge and four of his family lay buried I cannot remember; I think it must have been in '56 or '57, but whenever it may have been, it was a moment of shock. Above the crypt, if such it can be called (for it was once part of an open burial ground) there now rose the high red Victorian chapel of Highgate School, and in the dusky darkness of this unused and exposed 'crypt' was a sunken vault down six worn steps and in a state of appalling neglect. It was the tomb of the Coleridge family. The inscribed stones on its face had dropped askew so that I was able to push my walking stick through gaps and touch the rotting wood of the coffins within; the floor around it, flagged with old unwanted tombstones, was little but a dump of rags, rubbish, and various junk which included cast-out school desks and discarded, rusting iron girders. Britain's greatest philosopher-poet lay amid the rubbish forgotten. My illustration following page 86 tells the story better than words.

> Clime of the unforgotten brave!

[sang Byron in *The Giaour*]

> Shrine of the mighty! Can it be
> That this is all remains of thee?

(I must, even in this unhappy context, interpose that when I showed this picture, posed and used for our Appeal, to the irrepressible Pamela, she said that its only possible caption was, 'Call yourself a Laundry!')

A campaign, three years long, followed this visit, but I will not tire you with the legal difficulties that had to be overcome, and the long delays between one application and the next, to civil, municipal, and ecclesiastical authorities; it is enough to say that early in '61 we were ready. We had the approval of Coleridge's descendants and all the licences and 'faculties' necessary to remove the Coleridge coffins to a place of dignity. This was to be the centre of the nave, the very place of honour, in St Michael's Church, Highgate. St Michael's stands almost opposite Coleridge's last home in The Grove and was the church where he worshipped in the last year of his life; already it had on its walls a memorial tablet to him, erected by James and Ann Gillman, the devoted surgeon and his wife who had cared for him in their home, 3, The Grove, during his eleven last years when he lived 'in this hamlet'. The old Highgate chapel had been pulled down in 1833, and St Michael's succeeded it. Its vicar, Canon Edwards, his wardens and council gave us consent and every help; and in February '61 we launched our Appeal, the Society of Authors agreeing to act as its Treasurer and placing their offices and some of their staff at our service.

These are some of the words in the Appeal as published in the *Times Literary Supplement* and other literary journals.

'For many years it has been a matter of shock and grief to lovers of Coleridge, and to those who take a pride in our poetical heritage, that his tomb should remain in its present pitiable state—neglected, gaping, and partly surrounded by rubbish in a crypt that appears to be a dump for discarded iron, a receptacle for blown litter and leaves, and a convenient place for tramps to sleep in. This place was once the crypt of the old Highgate Chapel—' The words of this Appeal were mine, and I have since learned that here they are less than accurate. When the old chapel was torn down in 1833, its site was added to the burial ground that had adjoined it, and thus the Coleridge vault, from its building in 1834 when Coleridge died, lay under the open sky, 'in the old churchyard by the roadside', as Sara, Coleridge's daughter, said, who was destined to lie in the vault herself. If you walk to the very top of Highgate Hill, to the point where it begins to be the Great North Road, you will see this 'churchyard by the roadside' and if you can get past the padlock on its gate, as I once did, you can step down into the dark and open crypt and still see the sunken vault where Coleridge lay for a century and a quarter, from 1834 to 1961, when we took him away, his family with him, and decently sealed it up.

'Nobody,' my Appeal continued, 'seems to have known who owns the crypt or is responsible for it. Nobody has cared for it or for the sunken vault in its centre where Coleridge and his family lie. The facing and inscribed stones, which once hid the coffins of Coleridge and Sarah, his wife, have slithered down in the years, so that anyone who cares to can put his finger through the resulting cavities and touch the rotting wood of the coffins. . . . Also in the vault are the coffins of Coleridge's nephew, the nephew's wife (Sara, the poet's daughter), and their son.

'For two years and more a group of Coleridge lovers with the consent of Coleridge's descendants has been agitating to have these bodies removed to the dignity of St Michael's Church, Highgate . . . where they will lie in the centre of the nave beneath a slab inscribed with Coleridge's own epitaph:

> Stop, Christian passer-by. Stop, Child of God,
> And read with gentle breast. Beneath this sod
> A poet lies or that which once seemed he. . . .

'The costs of removal, building a new vault and having a fine stone inscribed are beyond the means of a private family, so a public appeal is being launched. . . . We earnestly commend this appeal. It has the support of distinguished Coleridge scholars here and in America who find it intolerable that the remains of one of our greatest poets should be left any longer as they are.'

This letter was signed by John Masefield, the Poet Laureate, Cecil Day-Lewis, John Betjeman, Richard Church, Christopher Fry, J. E.

Morpurgo (Director of the National Book League), Harold Nicolson, Kathleen Raine, the Mayor of St Pancras, the Lord Mayor of London, and myself.

The response in the first weeks was very friendly but slow. By April we had only £300 and, as always, the estimates of cost had risen; but we travelled on in faith and hope—and anxiety. Already the work of building the new brick vault was in hand; already the Bishop of London had consented to dedicate the new tomb and the Poet Laureate to deliver the address; already we had bought a slab of Westmorland green stone, 'a little piece of Lakeland' for a Lake poet and had commissioned, at a cost of £300, Mr Reynolds Stone, probably the finest designer and engraver in England, to cut the long inscription; and already we had learned that new outer coffins would have to be made since the wood of the old ones crumbled at a touch, though mercifully the leaden caskets within stayed intact.

And we had, so far, but £300.

But then America woke up to what was happening, and with its usual grandeur sent its money speeding across the Atlantic and justified our trust in humanity. American professors and distinguished citizens sent their cheques in benevolent letters, some announcing that they would come to the Dedication Service. I published this stirring news, and England woke up too. It woke up and competed with America so that soon we had, not only enough money to meet every conceivable expense, but enough to give St Michael's an endowment of the tomb which would ensure its upkeep 'in perpetuity'.

And on 28th March 1961 the remains of Coleridge, his wife, daughter, son-in-law, and grandson were reverently taken from that dark and forbidding vault, placed in their new coffins, and put to rest in their new and honourable home.

§

Then it was June 6th and the afternoon of the Dedication Service. What happened was, as I said without hesitation above, 'beyond my dreams'. More than a thousand people poured into St Michael's Church. To say that it was 'literally packed to the roof' is more like the truth than these enthusiastic 'literallies' usually are because the church has high galleries which were filled with the girls from Channing School and the boys from Highgate School—and what a magnificent Niagara of young voices they poured down upon the adults crowded on the floor below, as they sang, 'Who would true valour see Let him come hither; One here will constant be, Come wind, come weather. . . .' It dragged tears to some eyes. In the congregation below, massed to the walls, were people of international fame, T. S. Eliot, Professor Earl Griggs, probably the world's greatest authority on Coleridge, from California University, the Librarians of Yale and Princeton Universities, Professor I. A. Richards representing Harvard University, Kathleen Raine representing Girton, Cambridge; representatives from Canadian Universities, from the Society of Authors, the Royal Society of Literature, the Keats–Shelley Memorial Association, the Wordsworth 'Dove Cottage Trust' and the Charles Lamb Society. As interesting as any, if little known, was a colonel of the 15th–19th King's Royal Hussars, formerly the King's Light Dragoons, in which Coleridge, fleeing from Jesus, Cambridge, and seeing in a shop-window a recruiting poster for 'a few smart lads for the 15th Light Dragoons' enlisted under the name of 'Silas Tomkyn Comberbacke' (S.T.C.), only to have his discharge procured for him by shocked members of his family a few months later. Many of the poet's direct descendants were at the service, including his great grandson, Walter Henry Coleridge; Lady Coleridge who flew over from Paris; and three-year-old Josephine Coleridge, great-great-great-great-grand-daughter. The Mayors of Hornsey, St Pancras, and Hampstead represented their boroughs in the foremost pew.

Venerable and remarkable figures, when clergy and choir entered, were the Bishop of London in cope and mitre and the Poet Laureate in his doctoral robes, but I was told by some of the Americans that, impressed as they were by bishop and laureate, what stirred them most was another figure. In 1791 Coleridge had been a 'senior Grecian' in the Bluecoat School, Christ's Hospital, and now, after Bidding and psalm, there came up into the pulpit a tall boy in the traditional long sixteenth-century 'blue coat', with white bands, belt, and yellow stockings, a 'senior Grecian' too, and a successor of Coleridge after exactly a hundred and seventy years. He was come to read the traditional Speech Day lesson of his school, and fearlessly, clearly, beautifully—they are trained so to read it at Christ's Hospital—this boy, John Daniel, spoke the words of Jesus the Son of Sirach to our huge congregation: 'Let us now praise famous men, and our fathers that begat us. The Lord hath wrought great glory by them through his great power from the beginning.' The congregation was rapt into silence by the appropriateness of the old words to this occasion. 'Leaders of the people by their counsels, and by their knowledge of learning meet for the people, wise and eloquent in their instructions; such as found out musical tunes and recited verses in writing. . . . Their seed shall remain for ever, and their glory shall not be blotted out. Their bodies are buried in peace, but their name liveth for evermore. The people will tell of their wisdom, and the congregation will show forth their praise.'

Then followed Wesley's anthem, 'Thou shalt keep him in perfect peace', and a second lesson read by the Rev. Anthony Derwent Coleridge, great-great-grandson of the poet. Then while we all sang Bunyan's 'To be a pilgrim'—who could do other with those hundreds of children inspiring them from on high?—the Bishop and clergy proceeded to the new tomb. After the dedication came an anthem specially composed by Ivor Davies, the organist of the church, and sung by the Highgate School choir; the words being the familiar verse from Coleridge's *Ancient Mariner*, 'He prayeth well, who loveth well, Both man and bird and beast.'

Next the Poet Laureate's address. Eighty-six years old, his voice frail but still beautiful, he reviewed for us Coleridge's life and works and sufferings, and concluded, 'What more can I say of him? His poetry is the perfection of simple verse. There is nothing like it. The power of such simplicity cannot be described, and we can say of those stirring times no man was so gifted as Coleridge. He was a creature apart.'

The service over, many of us poured out through the evening sunlight of June and into the garden of the house where Coleridge had lived and died, 3, The Grove, Highgate, James and Ann Gillman caring for him there till the end. Here its present owners, Sir Mark and Lady Turner, had spread a lavish celebration party.

A LEGAL AFTERTHOUGHT

'Nobody seems to have known who owns the crypt or is responsible for it. Nobody has cared for it or for the sunken vault in its centre.' The first of these sentences may seem, on the face of it, an incredible statement, carelessly and improperly published in the national press after a too hurried study of the facts. And yet . . . I owe to Professor

Earl Griggs, whom I have called 'probably the world's greatest authority on Coleridge', and who was actively interested, like the scholar he is, in the old neglected tomb directly he heard of the proposed Reburial, the following scholarly notes.

'Inquiries made by several newspaper representatives also failed to fix the responsibility for the maintenance of the Coleridge vault. A writer in the *Evening Standard* of 27th January 1960, for example, reported that "Highgate School was clearly free from blame since it does not own the land". The same writer also quoted the senior assistant solicitor of the Hornsey Borough Council: "We have the care of the graveyard but not of the crypt in which Coleridge lies". A year later the *Hornsey Journal* of 24th February 1961 reported: "With the closing of the burial ground its upkeep became the responsibility of Hornsey Borough Council, but the council have always maintained that the part of the burial ground which was incorporated in the crypt is no longer a part and therefore not their responsibility. The school, on the other hand, maintain that they never took over the tomb—"'

Interrupting the Professor for a minute, I must submit I found it odd that when we informed the school that we proposed to dismantle the vault and remove the coffins, they said they were agreeable to this 'provided we left the crypt clean and tidy afterwards', which, since they had denied any obligation to the crypt under their chapel, seemed a condition hardly justified. *Ultra vires*, in fact. And what about all those unwanted school-desks cast out into this convenient cellarage for rubbish and junk? And, further, is it not a matter of wonder that a great public school, with a high record of scholarship, could have had the tomb of a famous English philosopher, scholar, and poet under its chapel and openly accessible from its forecourt and yet had never sent any of its sixth-form boys to make its environment clean, tidy, and worthy—a task which the boys, I am sure, would have set about with a will and a thrill; Coleridge lying among them as they worked.

But let me also remember that the school behaved well in providing the choir for the dedication of a better tomb.

The Professor, indefatigable, undefeatable, proceeds: 'A recent inquiry addressed to the Hornsey Borough Council in 1963 brought a more definitive answer from the Town Clerk: "Following the closing of the churchyard on the 4th July 1857: the churchwardens—and subsequently the Parochial Church Council—were responsible for its maintenance, and the Hornsey Borough Council have not at any time been so responsible."

So there it is. It's not for me to adjudicate who wins. Perhaps no one wins. Perhaps all the participants in this controversy can argue that 'churchyard' refers only to the open area remaining after a part of it got covered by the school chapel, which part became thereby a No-Man's-Land, a poor wounded name, with no bosom anywhere to lodge it. Anyhow, in the face of all this, I think I can claim that my words in the Appeal sorted well with the facts. And I cannot help wondering, after hearing all the experts, whether—should a tramp well-read in the Law make himself a lasting and somewhat smelly bivouac in that dark crypt on the crown of Highgate Hill—Council, School, Church, Government, or anyone else on earth, would possess the right to bid him take up his bed and walk.

3

BRANDHOEK BY YPRES

The next year, '62, yields a memory even more poignant, because more fully personal, than this triumphant reinterment of Coleridge.

That year I was dreaming of a novel that should be a study of the 'Old Boys' who still, after forty-five years wandered back to Ypres where they'd had their share in the First, Second, and Third Battles of Ypres; Ypres I, Ypres II, or Ypres III. Nowadays some of them wandered back alone, because the years were passing and people could be bored by their memories of that old receding war, and it was as well to keep quiet about it, even though the word 'Ypres' held for them the greatest experience of their lives, the most dreadful and yet the most wonderful thing that ever happened to them. For many all their subsequent years had been a little humdrum, empty of excitement, adventure, drama, terror, and offering never again those occasional sips from the strong wine of heroism.

My share was in Ypres III, the Battle for Paschendaele, so I returned to Ypres in October, because it was the autumn months of 1917 which had seen that deathly business, and its climax at last in the capture of Paschendaele. Like any other of the 'old sweats' revisiting the glimpses, I wandered along the Menin Road between the tall poplars, my eyes sweeping the country north and south of it, because all this had been the Salient. 'The Salient': these words are enough for us. It was now a green landscape lifting and swelling on either side, some parts of it rich pasture with the cows at rest or grazing, other parts a fat arable luxuriating with broad and leafy plantations of marigolds, tobacco, and beet. Small woods, grown tall in fifty years, stood here and there amid the well-farmed land. When I had come to it, all those years ago, it had been a grey tundra of viscous mud and glistening shell-ponds stretching over the visible world with splintered tree-trunks rising from it, none of them higher than a gibbet on which a man could hang. In '17 it had been this macabre grey limbo and moon-landscape; now it was a green, pleasant and flourishing country; but was there a square yard in all this area between sky and sky where a man had not suffered or died?

Swinging my eyes north and south of the road, after I'd passed Hell Fire Corner, I recognized place after place whose names haunt the memories of us all: to the north Potijze, Wieltje, Pilkem Ridge; to the south Zillebeke, Sanctuary Wood, Hill 60. It was while I surveyed the southern side that I recalled how, somewhere there, my wife's father, a lieutenant in the Royal Garrison Artillery, had been killed only a few weeks before I in my turn came to the Salient. None of Diana's family had ever known the true story of his death, or where his grave might be, or if he had a grave.

There are more than a hundred and thirty British Army cemeteries, all round Ypres and its Salient, some of them deep in the country, but I wondered if, while I was here, I could find trace of him in one of these. So in the morning I went to the Ypres Office of the Commonwealth War Graves Commission, and here their devoted servants—has anyone ever sung the superb, gracious, unwearying labours of our War Graves Commission through fifty years?—searched and searched for me among their innumerable shelved ledgers which hold a million names. At last, as I stood by a little Flemish clerk, looking over his shoulder while his finger travelled down the names, it stopped. 'Young, Lieutenant William Thomas, 12th Heavy Bty. Royal Garrison Artillery. Killed in action 12th July 1917. Age 36, 1. N. 3.

'It is here,' he said in fair but foreign English. 'I have it here. This is the register of Brandhoek Military Cemetery.... 1. N. 3—that is the location. The grave is in Plot 1, Row N, Grave 3.'

'But Brandhoek ?' I asked. 'Where is Brandhoek?'

'It is about half-way along the road between Ieper (Ypres) and Poperinghe, a few kilometres after Vlamertinge. You know the road? The main road?'

Did I not? What elderly man in Britain does not know that road? Had not five million British and Overseas troops come marching along it to the Salient? Did I not come up it with my brigade in '17 and sleep the night in a ruined barn at Vlamertinge where we broke our journey? Coming that way, had I then passed close to the grave of the man who, twenty-three years later, would be as a father-in-law to me (though I now am far older than he was then)? The road from 'Pop' and 'Vlam' to 'Wipers'. I set out at once for Brandhoek, and hardly a yard of that long straight Ypres-to-Poperinghe road but was a spring of memories that set the heart shaking. I passed through Vlamertinge trying to site the ruined barn where my sleep had been, and so, a little farther on, came to Brandhoek. No wonder I had not noticed it in '17 when I passed by, even if it was still standing then; it is but a tiny village with a few houses, a shop, a school, and a church, all apparently rebuilt from the ground up. Yes, there were three British cemeteries about it, each lifting its Cross of Sacrifice against the sky. Three? The kindly Flemish clerk had given me a location for the grave, but had said only 'Brandhoek Military Cemetery'. He had not spoken of three.

I searched in one of them, passing slowly through the long serried ranks of white headstones. I searched it a second time: could '1. N. 3' be somehow wrong? I searched in another cemetery, looking again and again at every stone, and they were many, but nowhere was I successful, and I began to fear lest I should fail in my mission. I so longed to find that grave. I longed to hurry back to Ypres and cable its discovery to Diana. Diana had never known her father who was killed when she was only a year old, but she had always felt a loyalty to his memory and believed that her love of books and literature, and her need to write books of her own, derived from him. He had been Lecturer in English Language and Literature at London University and the author, or editor with Dover Wilson, of several books. *An Anthology of the Poetry of the Age of Shakespeare*, *Poems of Keats* and *A Primer of English Literature*. I could not bear to leave Brandhoek unsuccessful.

I went into the third cemetery, peered and pried along the graves—where was 'Plot 1' and 'Row N'?—and then, suddenly, in a wonderful moment, I saw I was looking down at a headstone: 'Lieutenant W. T. Young, Royal Garrison Artillery, 12th July 1917.' It was in the front row of all, the third grave from the central path, and so opposite the altar-shaped Stone of Remembrance. Most beautifully kept, it had flowers springing at its foot, and the turf around it as trimmed and weedless as an Oxford lawn. For forty-five years, unknown to us, and we unknown to them, the Commission had looked after it for us, and kept it beautiful. A Belgian gardener was working among the graves, and I went to congratulate him on the grass, the flowers, and the scrupulous care of the headstone; and he told me in broken English that the Commission encouraged its foreign gardeners to plant the flowers they liked best in the way they liked best. I turned and saw how they all varied in style and planning along the different rows.

It was difficult to draw myself away from that gravestone, but I longed to get my message to Diana, and after one—and two—more glances at it, and at the whole cemetery with the foreign gardener tending the graves of British soldiers who fell before he was born, I returned to Ypres. I returned thinking there could be little doubt that her father had been brought from a temporary grave to this beautifully ordered cemetery, but how far that temporary grave had been from Brandhoek, and from the long straight road when I in my turn marched by, I could not know.

But when I was back in England, and we were making further inquiries, the Librarian of the War Office Library, which is no less gracious than the War Graves Commission, wrote to Diana, in formal language but feelingly, 'I have now had the opportunity to examine the War Diary of the 13th Heavy Brigade, R.G.A. The battery in which your father was serving, 12th Heavy Battery R.G.A., came under the command of 13th Heavy Brigade on 5th July. Both the Brigade and the Battery were stationed in the vicinity of Vlamertinge, a small village about five kilometres west of Ypres. I regret that the War Diary contains nothing which throws any light upon the circumstances in which your father was killed. The only reference to Lieut. W. T. Young is contained in a nominal roll of casualties suffered during the month; in no case is any additional information of officers' deaths given. From the War Diary it is apparent that your father's Battery was daily engaged in the shelling of German gun-batteries. It is, I think, reasonable to conclude that your father was killed by German counter-battery shelling, but I am afraid I can offer no proof of this. I very much regret that I am unable to give you any more detailed information about your father's death.'

The *Daily Express* published a brief story about my search and my tribute to the War Graves Commission, and as a result of this I received a letter from a patient in a Nottingham hospital.

'Dear Sir,

Reading the Daily Express of 6/11/62 I was greatly surprised to read of Lieutenant Young an Officer of the Artillery of which I served at the Battle of Paschendaele July 1917. I was in that battle and saw his dead body. He was buried at the foot of the Ridge along with many more for the time being. He was killed outright when a German shell heavy 9 point 2 hit the Gun pit killing all the Gun crew. I was in front serving on an 18 pounder Gun Royal Artillery, a direct hit on our gun killed most of our Gun crew. I was blown into a shell crater very deep one. Paschendaele was the Bloodyst Battle ever known, we lost enormous number of men the Germans was on the high ridge we at the bottom of the Ridge. I had spoken to Lieutenant Young the night before the battle as I was dispatch Orderly and he signed my book that gave orders from the Divisional Commander. I last saw him laid out on a stretcher along with another gallant officer Lieut. Holt, son of the Shipping Liner people. My address is as above, I am 66 years of age and in an ex-workhouse known as Hospitals today. I am quite fit and well but have nowhere else to live like many more men here. Well I will end my letter hoping I may see you some day with all my deep sympathy he was a great and brave officer believe me.'

At home we decided to let the winter pass and go to Brandhoek in the spring. It was a May day when we set off, and early in the evening when we arrived at Ypres. Intending to go to Brandhoek in the morning, we had a long summer evening in which I could introduce Diana to the Salient. The sun was dropping towards Paschendaele and illuminating the whole area with a light that seemed suitable to acres ever sacred to British eyes. We walked along the Menin Road between the blown poplars and over the pavé whose setts had known the feet of the young men, five million of them during those years '14 to '18. Diana has always said that this first sight of the Salient under a lovely shadow-flinging light was one of the two most memorable things in her life—the other being when, some years later, we walked along the Valley of the Brook Kidron into the Garden of Gethsemane. So deep were her feelings on both these first sights of places haunted for ever by a historic and world-changing pain that it was as if Time for a while were a stillness or had ceased to exist; as if some experiences can dwell in a dimension outside Time and different from those of every day. She knew that, in my day and her father's day, this Salient had been a tumbled sea of mud and water with slaughtered tree-boles rising everywhere from it, whereas now, on this late spring day, it was all young wheat and barley and flax prospering abundantly in squared fields as if nowhere in the world was there a richer soil to nourish them. In the far distance behind a grove of trees rose a single spire; a new-made spire; Paschendaele.

Thoughts too deep for tears.

I took her to Railway Wood—Railway Wood now a mass of lofty

trees on its oval hummock, but in my time no more than a rounded cranium of mud supporting a few scarecrow stumps and covering, fifteen feet beneath the tree-roots, a whole system of galleries, lit by electric lamps, with orderly rooms, sleeping rooms, sick bays, head-quarters, latrines and dumps opening off them. Down there I had lived in a company headquarters, sleeping, if at all, on a wire bunk, and never once in two weeks removing my clothes, but reading in our few idle hours William James's *Psychology*.

Sometimes when the Salient was quiet (if it was ever quiet) I had come up for a breather and, on this road where we stood now, strolled to and fro, looking very much the traditional hero, because I had gathered a small head-wound, so small that it involved only an inoculation against tetanus but did provide me with a handsome bandage all round my head and protruding honourably beneath my steel helmet. No traces anywhere now of the steep adits which had led down to those electrically lit corridors and offices under the earth. I suppose forty years of silt had occupied stairs and galleries and rooms. Perhaps here and there the deep roots of these crowding trees embraced the timbers of their broken roofs—I don't know.

The same beneficent sun was there for us in the morning when we waited at a bus station whose signboard said Vlamertinge, Brandhoek, Poperinghe, as if these were ordinary names. For Diana the bus-journey, so commonplace to the other passengers with their bags and baskets, was a blend of anticipation, happiness, and something like fear—perhaps 'awe' is the word; awe at an appointment with some-thing strange and sweet but a little troubling. All her childhood she had played with make-believe dreams of her father coming back, not dead, but living, and her seeing him for the first time. All her girlhood, when fascinated by some older man—a film actor as likely as not—her thought had been, not 'How wonderful to have him as a lover' but 'as a father'; and now she was going to stand but a few feet from where her father lay.

Brandhoek. We alighted and walked through the tiny village to the third of its war cemeteries. The cemetery was quiet between its square of trimmed hedges and empty except for the Belgian who was at work again among the flowers. I led her to the grave, and when we had looked at it for a while, with the flowers of May around it now, pansies, violas and gillyflowers, salvia, lobelia, and yellow musk, I left her there and walked with my camera to a distance, knowing that this was an hour of which we would want a lasting picture. I took the photograph which appears here.

It is a good photograph, and says, I think, enough.

§

Most of the smaller countries and cities of Europe will give a welcome and full help to any author who purposes to write a book about them. The City of Ypres was an instant example of this. Every help was promised to this English novelist who wished to write a novel about the 'Old Survivors' of the city's immortal days. A Monsieur Roland Annoot at the Town Hall declared enthusiastically, 'Anything we can do we will of course do, but the one man in Ypres who can really give you all you need is Docteur Vétérinaire Caenepeel-Daelman. There is nothing, absolutely nothing, he doesn't know about the Salient and Paschendaele and all the battles for Ypres. He has every book written about any of these, no matter what its language.' M. Annoot lifted his telephone, spoke in it, and told us we could go and see Dr Caenepeel at once. We hastened to his house near the abattoir where his work lay, and what a welcome he gave us in the small room walled with shelves of books about Ypres (including even one of mine and one of Gilbert Frankau's, Pamela's father). It was the welcome, with port and biscuits, of a man overjoyed to have in his study two persons who would share with him the major interest of his life. Dr Caenepeel could not have been much over forty years old, and as this was 1963, he was barely born, if born at all, in 1914–18, but 'Ypres in 1914–18' were the magical words for him. Why, yes, he would finish at the abattoir by noon, and if we would return, he would give all his day to us, taking us to any place which would be of any help to M'sieur in his book, and to the area south of Brandhoek where the 12th Battery of the Royal Garrison Artillery must have been, and where Madame's father would have fallen by his guns.

So that afternoon, with the sun still pronouncing its benediction over the Salient, Dr Caenepeel took us in his excitable little car at continental speed (which saves time) hither, thither, northward, southward, to any place of stirring interest and deep appeal among these fields and woods and pastures: to Sanctuary Wood with its magnificent Canadian memorial where an avenue of maple trees from Canada leads to the beautiful rose-parterres, stepped tier after tier as if to speak with ever-mounting power of Canada's sorrow and Canada's praise; to Zonnebeke and Polygon Wood; to Gheluvelt and Hooge; to Tyne Cot Military Cemetery, largest in the world, with 12,000 buried there and 35,000 names of the missing inscribed on long white panels. Some of the white headstones here bore as their only inscription, 'An Unknown British Soldier. Known to God' or, no less cared for, 'An Unknown German Soldier. Known to God.' Then to Langemark and its huge German cemetery, where 30,000 lie, and there is a mass-grave of 24,000; and so at last into Paschendaele itself, a little village rebuilt on its once (for us) murderous and unconquerable Ridge.

Astonishing the contrast between the white British cemeteries where each soldier has his own headstone with his rank, name and the insignia of his regiment, and that German cemetery at Langemark, stern, solemn, oppressive in its solemnity, where every grave was but a small metal number in the grass and the low black crosses stood at sternly regimented intervals, unrelated to any individual among the dead. If ever a place has seemed haunted to me it was this large field of death with those low black crosses severely distanced from one another; those tall overshadowing trees severely ordered too; and the absence of all names—the names of the numbered dead had to be sought in the registers at the grim, square entrance-building. Here one seemed to be standing in a greyer world than anywhere else in the Salient. Was it our imagination that everything here symbolized the minor importance of individual men compared with the authoritarian State? Surely an alien culture embraced us. As we stepped out of the Langemark cemetery, the sun seemed brighter over the Belgian fields, and the air easier.

When Dr Caenepeel had shown us all the Salient between Langemark and Ypres, he took us to level fields south of Brandhoek and here stopped the car near a farmhouse and a crossroads. Somewhere near here, he thought, the 13th Heavy Brigade must have been, and the 12th Heavy Battery of Madame's father.

We wandered about these quiet and empty fields for a while.

Then, to crown all—and crown is the suitable word—when we were back in Ypres, M. Annoot in the Town Hall allowed us to climb with Dr Caenepeel up through gallery after gallery to the belfry of the Cloth Hall's great central tower, with its carillon of bells and so on to the battlemented summit beneath its 'helmet' lantern.

This was a moment almost beyond my mind's acceptance. In my first volume I have described how on an evening in 1917 I came marching through the rubble and ruins of Ypres 'past the cascaded tower of the Cathedral and the pallid fangs of the Cloth Hall'. The central tower of the Cloth Hall was then but a broken and hollowed tooth standing only a little higher than the Hall's shattered wings on its either side. As I marched by, that evening, I remembered an evening in my theological college, five years before, when our Principal, giving us a lecture on the Medieval Gothic, threw on his screen a picture of the Great Cloth Hall of Ypres in all its thirteenth-century majesty, its many-windowed façade four hundred and forty feet long, its tower rising from its midst to a height of two hundred and fifty feet. It was, he had said, 'the most famous example of municipal Gothic in the world and an amazing tribute to the power of Flemish trade and commerce in this, the "City of Cloth"'. And here it lay, on this evening of 1917, five years later: four hundred and forty feet of continuous rubble-heaps with a few jagged fragments of wall rising from among them, and the shards of its tower hardly six feet taller. But now—1963—my wife and I were standing on the crenellated summit of that tower, arisen again, and no different in any detail from what it had been seven hundred years before.

I looked down at the Grand' Place of Ypres far below, where the pavé cobbles over which we had marched still lay; then I walked round the 'helmet' and gazed over the whole of the Salient. I looked at it all for a long time—but not so long as the old British lion, couched on the summit of the Menin Gate Memorial, who gazes out at the Salient for ever.

Diana inevitably looked southwards to the flat green fields near Brandhoek. The part she wanted to see was easy to find because it was near the broad expanse of the Dikkebus Lake ('Dicky-bush' to us in the old days). On this clear evening the view was so vast that we could see Poperinghe ten miles away at the end of the long road and even, northward, the sea. The sea where stood Ostend and Blankenberghe and Zeebrugge which Third Ypres had battled to reach, but never did. The low ridge of Paschendaele, with its spire yonder, stopped that.

So deep was the impression made upon Diana by the Ypres Salient that next day we hired a car and visited all the great places again, so that we could stand among them, dreaming. The final fruit of these days in the Salient was a novel by Diana, *The Noonday Sword*, a remarkable book, as I and many disinterested critics have declared, to come from a woman's hand. It is dedicated to her father, and the whole of its Part II covers the Third Battle of Ypres, under an epigraph which are words from a poem by E. A. Mackintosh, an Old Pauline like myself, who fell in action in October, '17. They are 'Underneath the open sky . . . Lads, you're wanted. Come and die'.

On our last night we went, of course, at nine in the evening, while it was still but summer dusk, to the Menin Gate for the daily ceremony there. The Menin Gate Memorial is a pillared and classical archway, a hundred feet long, spanning the Menin Road. On its white walls are cut the names of 50,000 British dead whose bodies were never found. Its inscription, beneath the British lion who watches over the Salient for ever, runs 'To the Armies of the British Empire who stood here from 1914 to 1918 and to Those of their Dead who have no known Grave'. Towards nine o'clock the police halt all traffic through the Arch, and as the hour chimes from the churches and the Cloth Hall two of the City's young firemen, facing inward upon the archway and the 50,000 names, raise silver bugles to their lips and sound Britain's 'Last Post'. We stood there to listen, next to two men who looked English and elderly and were doubtless old veterans like the stranger at their side. They sprang to attention as the first note rang out beneath the archway's high coffered roof, and so remained, still and very erect, till the last note died away.

It is fitting, I think, that I should end this chapter with the closing paragraph of the novel which I did, in the end, write about the Old Survivors of Ypres, since I am one of them.

'It is said that the soldiers of the old armies, while finding words, often unseemly, for the singing music of other bugle calls, never touched with any ribaldry the Last Post, the call that ends the day. As "Parade" sang out, they might say or think, "Fall in A. Fall in B. Every bloody companee." To "Defaulters" if happily it was not summoning them, they might apply the serene words, "You can be a defaulter As long as you like, As long as you answer your name," and to "Retreat" which sings the sun down, "You won't go to Heaven when you die, Mary Ann", but to the Last Post no words at all because it is too beautiful; nothing; only silence and reverence. All the same, when at the end it sounds its two lengthened notes, some have chosen to hear the words "Lights out. . . . Lights out . . ." or "Come home. . . . Come home. . . . Are ye there? . . . Are ye there?"

4

MYSTERY AT PILTDOWN

It was soon after I had built myself a cottage in Cuckfield, Sussex, in the year 1923, that I met Sir Arthur Smith Woodward, one of the greatest geologists in Britain, and, indeed, in the world. To list his medals, prizes and distinctions it would be necessary to mention almost every country in the world. He had dug for fossils and done other palaeontological research in both hemispheres, and north, south, east, and west. He had been Keeper of the Geological Department in the British Museum, President of the Geological Society; of the Linnean Society; and of the Palaeontographical Society. When I first met him he was in his early sixties, a tall man whose neat white beard, fine bald domed head, and grave manner made him the very picture of an illustrious scholar. His was a noble presence.

With his wife, Lady Maud, and Margaret, his only child, he lived in an attractive house, Hill Place, near Haywards Heath, a mile or so from my home in Cuckfield. Just as I had made my home in Sussex because I loved its broad Weald and its high Downs, so he had come to live there permanently for the sake of a patch of gravel.

This patch of gravel was near a village hardly worth a mark on a map, but whose name now echoed all over the world. As Sir Arthur used to say to me, 'I have met people in the Americas and China who have never heard of Brighton or even of Sussex, but they've all heard of Piltdown.' They probably hear of it and talk of it still because, if it has lost the original cause of this international fame, it now enshrines the diverting story of a fraud that for forty years deceived nearly all the scientists of the world. And something unworthy in us delights to see these great scholars, these formidable, expert, indisputable authorities, proved to be fallible creatures like ourselves.

One day in 1908 a Lewes solicitor, Mr Charles Dawson, who was also a devoted, learned, and locally famous amateur geologist, wandering over Fletching and Piltdown commons, saw some workmen digging up gravel for a new driveway, and he, with the eye of an expert, detected at once from the smoothness, rounding, and colour of the stones, that they had been subject to the action of running water; but nowadays the Sussex Ouse, draining this catchment-area, flows along a valley far below Fletching and Piltdown, so it was obvious, to Mr Dawson's expert eye that this gravel must belong to a date ages before water action, after the disappearance of the dome of chalk that used to join North Downs to South Downs, had uncovered the Weald as we know it now. Assessing a date for the water-washing of this gravel as belonging to several hundred thousand years ago, he approached the workmen and said, 'If you come across anything odd in this gravel, anything that looks like bones perhaps, put it aside for me.'

Well, sure enough, a few days later one of the men came across something odd. It looked rather like a 'brown old coconut' (Sir Arthur's words to me) so the foreman, or the discoverer, said, 'I wonder if this could be what that old codger meant,' and, picking up a sledge-hammer, he brought it down on the top of the coconut to learn more—and away into pieces went the world-famous Piltdown skull. That, at least, was how Sir Arthur would tell the story to me, but I have a suspicion, since reading some of the endless literature on Piltdown Man, that there was some gay guess-work, picturesque improvement, or even a too easy credulity here. When Charles Dawson next appeared at the site, the men showed him a piece, and he suggested, to the men and later to the world, that this might prove a world-shaking discovery, because here was probably the brain-case of a creature half-ape and half-man.

Of course he and other enthusiastic geologists dug and dug in the gravel pit but it was not till a day in 1911 that Dawson found another piece of the same skull. In time the searchers were rewarded by finding in the darkest deeps of the gravel the bones of ancient or extinct rhinoceros and hippopotamus and mastodon, some flint implements, a curious tool made of elephant bone and—above all—a jaw-bone simian in character but apparently of the same date of fossilization as the skull. Controversy now rocked the scientific world: did the jaw-bone belong to the skull? If so—and at first another Sir Arthur, Sir Arthur Keith, President of the Royal Anthropological Institute, decided that it did so belong—then there had slouched amid our Sussex herbage a sub-human creature who was neither Pithecanthropus erectus nor True Man. Eoanthropus dawsoni he was dubbed, the Dawn Man of Mr Charles Dawson.

More cautiously, Sir Ray Lankester, then Professor of Zoology and Comparative Anatomy in the University of London, maintained a lifelong doubt about the jaw's relation to the skull. All he would allow in a fascinating letter to H. G. Wells was, 'I think we are stumped and baffled. The most prudent way is to keep jaw and cranium apart in all argument about them. On the other hand, on the principle that hypotheses are not to be multiplied beyond necessity, there is a case for regarding the two—jaw and cranium—as having been parts of one beast—or man.'

Smith Woodward, more confident, almost wholly confident that jaw and cranium belonged together, was associated from the first, both as an old friend and as the British Museum's expert, with Charles Dawson at the Piltdown site, and digging with them in the years 1912 and 1913 was a young French Jesuit who was also geologist and palaeontologist, by name Father Pierre Teilhard de Chardin, known forty years later to men of science all over the world, and to a huge lay public, by his book, *The Phenomenon of Man*; indeed it was Teilhard de Chardin who on 30th August 1913 found the all-important canine tooth. When further fragments of extinct animals were dug up the place became almost the dominating interest of Sir Arthur's life. He came to live in Hill Place so as to be near Piltdown and to be able to continue digging. In a place of honour in his Hill Place dining-room hung a large rectangular picture of a stumpy, naked, hairy, monkey-faced man crouching onwards by the reeds of a river—presumably the prehistoric waters of our Sussex Ouse. From the water emerged a hippopotamus to snarl at this naked hunter with his tools.

It is amusing, now that we all know the shocking last chapter of this story, to read in Wells's *Outline of History* (1920): 'Upon these fragile Piltdown fragments more than a hundred books, pamphlets, and papers have been written. These scraps of bone are guarded more carefully from theft and wilful damage than the most precious jewels, and in the museum cases one sees only carefully executed fac-similes.'

Sir Arthur would thrill me as he related, with no little drama, Dawson's moment of staggering discovery, or talked of his own labours at the gravel pit with him, or unrolled his ideas about the nature, character, and habits of his Dawn Man. Glancing round at the picture behind him of the hairy man in the reeds by the river, he would tell how once, lecturing on Eoanthropus in Lewes he showed a slide of Piltdown Man's probable head and face with low brow, flat nose, chinless, ape-like jaw, and canine tooth overlapping a thick lip, only to meet a man from the audience afterwards who declared that he found the picture quite unremarkable because 'you could meet chaps like that in Lewes any day'.

Knowing how, though it was now eighteen years since Dawson's first discovery, he would still go to dig and dig in that gravel—such is the tireless perseverance of a true scientist—I begged to be allowed to accompany him one day and to dig too. He consented at once. 'Of course come. There's nothing I'd like better than to have a navvy to help. It's a lonely job.'

Excited, I called for him one morning with my car, a small Wolseley with a dicky behind, into which this distinguished man loaded a common kitchen sieve, a pick, spades and a bucket. I motored him, if my memory is right, along a rough road through Scaynes Hill to some high ground near Fletching Common, where he said abruptly, 'Stop here. Stop here and I'll explain everything.'

We got out, he looked to see if I was safely beside him, and began his explanation with seven words that opened for me, as never before, a window into the mind of a geologist. He pointed first to the shadow of the North Downs, swinging along the sky across the vastness of the Weald, and then to our steep South Downs rolling along behind us, and said, 'All this, of course, is modern stuff.'

That our beloved South Downs, our minor mountains of Sussex, our 'everlasting hills', should be dismissed as modern stuff! But his mind was way back in geological ages 'before the hills in order stood Or earth received her frame'; before the waters washed an ever-widening trough between North and South Downs and, uncovering the gault, the greensand, and the wealden clay, spread like a table before us this rich and lovely Weald, all blue-misted ploughland, woodland, and pasture. He directed my eyes to the Ouse now flowing far below the water-worn gravel which we were about to visit.

And so to Piltdown. I was excited to see the small gravel pit beneath a hedge that bordered a roadway. It looked little bigger than a circular hollow dug by playing children in a corner of their garden. But this, of course, was nearly twenty years after the first discovery.

Our morning's work demonstrated yet further to me the patient, obstinate, undefeatable perseverance with which a scientist pursues his research in all the modesty of loneliness. Sir Arthur, with shirt-sleeves rolled back to the elbows, insisted on every spadeful of gravel which he or I lifted being slowly strained through the sieve, while he peered at it to see if there was 'anything there'. Much he scanned through a magnifying glass. And this though he had been digging here fruitlessly for years. The only fossil we unearthed throughout the morning was a trilobite which he looked at, laughed at, and after explaining it as palaeozoic tossed away as common and uninteresting.

Ah well, that was in the twenties. In the fifties, years after Sir Arthur had died still believing in his Dawn Man, 'the Earliest Englishman' as he would call him; forty and more years after Dawson's first discovery, years during which some sceptics had shaken their heads over the likelihood of an ape-like jaw and a sub-human brain-case belonging together; after, in 1949, another famous geologist, loaded with medals like Sir Arthur but fifty years younger than he, had submitted the remains to a 'fluorine dating test' and other scientists to tests for nitrogen, carbon, sulphate, and collagen (some of which I can understand but most of which I can't, so seek no elucidation here) and all had decided that skull and jaw were of no great age; and after, in 1959 the bones had been subjected to 'radio-active examination' and 'carbon 4 dating' (again I leave it to you) it was finally proved to the world that cranium and mandible had been artificially but most learnedly stained with chromium and iron-sulphate solution to give them the appearance of fossilization; that the teeth of the jaw had been deliberately abraded with tools so as to look like 'worn' human teeth, such 'wear' not appearing in the teeth of apes; that the elephant-bone tool or club had been shaped by a modern knife; that, in short, the skull was that of a fairly recent human and the jaw that of an orang-utan. Both of which, together with the other exciting flints and tools and animal remains must have been carefully inserted at different times by a human hand into the gravels, and that the whole business was one scholarly and majestic fraud.

Any one of these testings proved the fraud; all and each of the others independently confirmed it.

The skull 'that of a fairly recent human': so the amateur listener to Sir Arthur Woodward's lecture at Lewes was not so far wrong when, unsurprised by a picture of 'Piltdown Man Reconstructed', he said, 'You can see chaps like that in Lewes any day.'

Mr J. S. Weiner, one of the scientists whose suspicions and investigations first exposed the fraud, in his enthralling (if occasionally, to the layman, unintelligible) detective-story, *The Piltdown Forgery*, expounding this creation of a composite man-ape, directs our minds to the sequence of well-made scenes in the admirable drama: the discovery of the ancient gravel, then the finding of a fossil cranium; then the unearthing of a mysterious jaw; and later that of the eye-tooth; then the convincing appearance of flint tools and animal bones to document the skull's authenticity and antiquity; and finally, in 1915, more fragments of a similar skull at some distance away.

He calls the subject of the play, 'the foisting of a spurious fossil human ancestor on to the world of palaeontology'.

One thing abundantly certain is that the perpetrator of this excellent fraud was an expert archaeologist, geologist, and palaeontologist with no small knowledge of chemistry, physics, and dental anatomy. And further that it must have been Someone There most of the time. Someone whose name has been mentioned in the endless monographs and papers written about Piltdown Man.

Two we can eliminate straightaway. One is Sir Arthur Smith Woodward. That there was a natural nobility about him I have already suggested; and any complicity in a fraud, except that of being deceived, is unthinkable. Besides, it has been established that he knew nothing about the Piltdown fragments till after they had been produced by Dawson. Moreover, I who worked at his side in 1926 know that he still believed passionately in the skull and was labouring in its interest twenty years after its first traces had been found.

The other is Fr Teilhard de Chardin who found the canine tooth in 1913. Apart from being a man of known sanctity, he left England for France the same year, and was away for years, but more 'authenticating' bones and implements were planted in 1914 and 1915.

(Is it unkind, is it even unjustified in this context to point out that Charles Dawson died in 1916 and nothing of interest happened at Piltdown after that. Who knows?)

Who the scholarly forger was remains one of the world's great mysteries, though, to my mind, deductions from possibility, probability, psychology and horse sense point steadily to one figure. Before whom I bow.

5

OF MOUNTAINS AND ROCKS

I have told this story here because it serves as the curtain-raiser to a chapter on my love for mountains and rocks.

Margaret Woodward, Sir Arthur's daughter, was in the habit of going yearly with a party of friends to the Swiss or Austrian mountains for winter sports, and in this year of '26 she asked me to be one of them. I accepted with enthusiasm though I had never gone ski-ing before. I bought skis at once, and she instructed me, so far as this was possible on the level lawns of her Hill Place garden in an elegant use of them. Margaret might be my instructor but she was much younger than I was, and when we set off for the mountains, Lady Woodward said laughingly, 'I put her entirely in your charge. Please bring her back safe. . . . And yourself too,' she added. 'Of course.'

On Christmas Eve of '26 our party, about forty of us, set off for Zürs in the Austrian Tyrol.

Zürs, is, or was then, a tiny Alpine village high up in the Vorarlberg mountains and consisting mainly of two wooden-built hotels, the Edelweiss and the Alpenrose, and a small chapel. Our large party divided itself between these hotels, Margaret and myself choosing the Alpenrose. Most were skiers of some expertness; I can remember only two of us who spent our first days on the 'nursery slopes', an attractive girl, Joyce Berridge, and myself. But she and I were happy enough together (she was a charming girl) while the others had gone off on 'expeditions' over the mountains. During these first days on easy slopes Joyce and I acquired some skill, and even elegance, in straight running (skis together and no tramlines), but usually fell badly, though jovially, when attempting to stop—or, worse, do a 'Christy' turn. Margaret was expert enough to go on expeditions with the skilled, so we saw little of her before dinner-time.

Then it was New Year's Day, 1927. Margaret went off with six others on an expedition to the summit of Mt. Valluga. It was told to us afterwards that all the visitors at Zürs had been warned not to venture across the new clean snow on that mountain because of a warm south wind prevailing, the Foehn, which, in alliance with the warm breath of an Alpine winter sun, could make the snow on a steep mountain-side shifty and treacherous. This could not have been a very forceful warning because a party of stalwart young Germans from the Edelweiss went up the mountain ahead of our party with a local instructor and guide. He may have reassured them that in mid-winter a warm spell can change overnight into frost and render the snow safe. Anyway he led the Germans, and our string of seven followed in their ski-tracks some hundred yards behind. Both parties had 'traversed' up much of the mountain-side when, according to an eye-witness in the valley below, a crack in the white snow, looking like a streak of black forked-lightning, shot across the steep slope for about half a mile, and a first avalanche came tearing down upon both parties, overthrowing them in their tracks—to be followed instantly by a far greater fall, 'a towering wall of snow twenty-five feet high' coming down with that terrible long thunder-sheet roar of an Alpine avalanche. 'Twenty-five feet high' may have been the exaggeration of an excited man, but all of our party were buried deep and lost to sight after the fall halted. So were a few of the Germans ahead and their guide instructor. These were killed. But other young Germans who had escaped the avalanche, or dug themselves out of it—I don't know which—came ski-ing down to where the 'English' had last been seen hoping to be of help. But nothing was visible on the mountain until at last one of them espied the tip of a ski protruding above the snow. Immediately, coming to it, they whipped out those metal ski-tips which experts carry as spare parts in case their ski-points break, and with these as their only spades they dug for nearly an hour and at length extricated Margaret still alive. Astonishing that one can breathe and live though buried deep under snow. Of course she was danger-ously frozen and these young Germans, experts and knowing what to do, pressed their bodies about her body to pour their warmth into her.

I have often thought that this simple scene, happening only a few years after the first War illustrated how the young of any nation are usually more eager to preserve life than to destroy it. Gently these young Germans helped her home.

You can enter into my thoughts when, after having heard the avalanche and received the news that our party had been overwhelmed, and after pacing up and down, up and down, remembering Lady Woodward's laughing words, 'Bring her back safely,' word came down the mountain that she at least had been saved.

All that afternoon and evening with the mid-winter dusk falling, it was a moving experience to watch the local rescue parties from Stuben, Lech, and Zürs itself assembling near the chapel under a captain's orders and then ascending the mountain one behind another, with all their saving equipment on their backs: braziers, fuel, torches, blankets, tents, and drawing sleighs behind them for stretchers. They were going to work at finding the buried and, if possible, healing the frozen, all through the last of the daylight and, with torches, through the night. But they found only the bodies of four of our companions, and brought them down and laid them in the little chapel.

Recovery of the other two had to be abandoned till the spring. Among the four dead was Maurice Rackham, brother of the artist, Arthur Rackham, and one woman, Cicely Penrose Foster. Their funeral was the strangest funeral I was ever to witness and have a share in. Four sleighs drawn by mules came to the chapel for the coffins, locally carpentered. All the men of our party in their mountain wear and with their skis on their feet stood waiting. The only way down to the village of Lech with its little church and churchyard was a narrow tilting track of hard frozen snow. The four sleighs with their burdens went first, and we, in single file, came slowly ski-ing behind them. In the few places where the way was steep we had to stem so as to maintain the slow pace and keep a proper interval between mourner and mourner. Our single file procession came in sight of Lech, and there we saw all the women of the village assembled in a line by the road, and wearing their black in mourning for our dead. They bent their heads as we ski-ed by. Beyond them, in a similar formal line, were the pompiers in their fire-fighting kit (come whence I know not) and these stood at attention till the last of us had passed. When we entered the small church-yard we saw that the four open graves were garlanded with evergreens, laid there by the local people. These local people, all in their decent black, followed quietly behind us. There was no Anglican clergyman to conduct the service up in the mountains here; there was only myself who had withdrawn from Orders a few years before. I had no Book of Common Prayer with me, but after eight years as a priest, four of them with the infantry in a murderous war, I knew the whole service by heart, every word of it, as an actor knows all the lines of some long Shakespearean role after a long run; and our party asked me to conduct the service for them. *The Times* in a full description of this funeral, built up, no doubt, from an Exchange message, said, 'The Service was conducted by a C. of E. minister, The Rev. Mr White of London.' It could not have been more wrong; even the old Thunderer can nod. It was conducted by one of the companions of the dead who was no longer a minister of the C. of E. and came, not from London, but from Sussex. At the head of the graves opposite me stood the Governor of the Province of Vorarlberg representing the Austrian Government. With him stood members of the Provincial Diet, the village fathers of Lech, and officers from some Tyrolese Sporting Clubs.

When I had spoken the service from memory and concluded it with the 'Grace' only, being no longer qualified to pronounce a Blessing, the Governor, a natural orator like so many mid-European statesmen, addressed us all on behalf of the Austrian Government and people. On the whole ours was a party of literary sophisticates who, ostensibly, 'had no use for' anything they could call sentimental, but it was obvious to me that some of them were responding to this gentle and exquisitely phrased valediction with invisible tears. I can call up out of the past only two things that he said. One was 'These our visitors, gallant and reckless, have paid the small toll which Nature exacts if others in their thousands are to return from our mountains to their homes in safety', and the other (his closing words, I think), 'They came as our guests and now they shall remain in our keeping for ever.'

It was over, and we filed out of the churchyard to climb the steep path to Zürs, either with our skis on our shoulders or wearing them on our boots with their seal-skins under them.

That was the last funeral I ever conducted. A service out of time.

Back in Zürs, we gathered together to consider what memorial we should erect over those graves, and what words they should bear. Our leader, Oswald Cox, found them for us. They were:

> Fear no more the heat o' the sun
> Nor the furious winter's rages,
> Thou thy worldly task hast done.

All our party went home immediately, except Margaret Woodward, Joyce Berridge, and myself. We stayed with Margaret till she should be strong and well again and have had a few more days on the snows, so as to recover her old joy in them.

§

My wife after our marriage was an easy convert to my love for mountains—she had climbed Snowdon with some of her seniors in the Ministry of Food when they were all evacuated to North Wales—and we have made for nearly thirty years now, our happy hunting-ground among the mountains of Cumberland and Westmorland. Our base has been Rosthwaite in Borrowdale from which access is easy to most peaks in the Cumberland massif, and where the Scafell Hotel is a charming home-from-home. Each year at the Scafell you are almost sure to find, among many strangers, the faces of long familiar friends, because the 'incurables' among mountain climbers—the 'recidivists' if you like—tend to return there year after year. Some of the rooms are even named after them.

'Climbers'? Well, to begin with, I am using that word to describe those who manage to get up Scafell Pike, the Gable, Glaramara, High Stile, and others by the normal method of locomotion, putting one foot in front of the other; and if to get to the summit of Scafell Pike, the highest mountain in England is not 'climbing' I don't know what is. But the austere rope-and-rock climbers will not allow this noble word to those who arrive on the tops by this commonplace method, having needed no rope at all; they are but 'walkers'. For a long time Diana and I were but walkers in the eyes of these great ones. But we did some strenuous things which, if not 'climbing' in the sense given to that word by people who live on the levels, Lord knows what they were.

The most memorable was an ascent of Scafell by Lord's Rake, the West Wall Traverse, and Deep Ghyll. Scafell is not Scafell Pike; it is the true peak of Scafell but forty feet lower than the Pike. The ascent of the Pike is easy; much less so the ascent of Scafell itself, and this Lord's Rake–Deep Ghyll route is probably the best way up its famous and fearsome North Face. Lord's Rake has a bad name but it is really quite unterrifying; it is a rocky, switchbacking corridor across the North Face—that stormy presence, all wrinkled with buttresses, fissures, and other black and hostile looks. More, the Rake is made tolerable for the nervous by frequent tall fragments of rock on the precipice side; and the thing to do, if nervous, is to go quickly from one of these to the next. The West Wall Traverse is a shelf beneath a blank slab but quite negotiable if—again—you step it quickly and don't look down. It leads you into Deep Ghyll which is a long steep wet 'chimney' going up and up till it delivers you on to the very summit of the mountain. Then, suddenly, the whole world is around you again, and the whole sky above you, and in your heart a sense of conquest better than most things on this earth. Diana and I and two good mountain friends, Dorothy and Peter Critchley (doctor and surgeon who might come in useful) were doing the climb up Deep Ghyll (nothing will induce me to call it a walk—a *walk*, for heaven's sake!) and I came last with Diana above me; she had said she would like to have me behind her so as to block the view if, by mistake or mischance, she looked down. She was climbing in slacks, and when I remember Deep Ghyll I always feel compelled to say that while in ordinary circumstances human posteriors are empty of expression, this is not true in a nerve-racking chimney high on a mountain; then they can register with quivers and grimaces all manner of anxiety, strain and doubt. My chief anxiety in Deep Ghyll was the way the rocks sweated with moisture as you sought fingerholds among them. Sometimes a portion of rock came away as I gripped it, and I hastily put it back lest its removal upset the architecture of the mountain. But that issue out of the dark constriction of Deep Ghyll on to the mountain's crown, with the high clean air and the spreading sunlight all around you, and a view of the world as far as the Irish Sea, is like nothing so much as Pluto issuing out of the mouth of Hell. We stood there glorying.

You should try it.

Then one morning Captain Badrock ('Sandy'), proprietor of the Scafell Hotel and a fine rock-climber on all the mountains around it, was driving three of us somewhere in his car, Diana, myself, and another of his guests, 'Tobit' Birt, a publisher then but later to become a distinguished Anglican priest. Of a sudden Sandy surprised us by asking, 'Why don't you take up proper climbing?'

Yes, 'climbing' he said, after Deep Ghyll. Proper climbing.

'You mean rock-climbing?' we asked.

'Of course. Come rock-climbing with me some time.'

We went with him that same afternoon, complete with ropes, slings, karabiners, and apprehension. He took us to the Glaciated Slab in Coomb Gill where the first climb is easy, a 'moderate' and others rather more difficult. Climbers grade the well-known climbs as Moderate, Difficult, Very Difficult, Severe, or Very Severe. Some like to add another grade, the Totally Impossibles, which are only achieved by the greatest tigers—such an Impossible as the one ascended for the first time in a mist by Leigh Mallory because he'd left his pipe somewhere above. Sandy led us up the Moderate on the Slab and then

up and down one which was at least called a Difficult. By the end of
that afternoon two of his three pupils were won. Tobit had done some
'climbing' before but the two Raymonds were converts, and fanatical
ones at that. Tobit was to become (as well as a parson) a far finer
climber than either of us. It should be recorded that a little before he
was ordained he did some difficult climbs so as to train himself to do
them in the future without swearing.

In the same valley, Coomb Gill, there is an odd and popular
climb known as 'Dove's Nest', and for some the most disturbing
feature of it is, not its height or steepness, but that at one place you
have to crawl upon your belly like a reptile through a twisting tunnel in
the dark heart of the rock. Sandy, who on these early climbs always
'led', stood at the entrance to this tunnel, an opening about the size
of one that lets a dog into its kennel, and said, 'Don't do this if you
don't want to. Just say if you'd rather not come.' Diana was second on
the rope, I third and last, and as I have a nightmarish horror of any
claustrophobic experience I stood hoping to hear Diana reply, 'No, I
don't think I'll come, Sandy,' which would justify me in saying, 'Well,
perhaps I'd better stay with Diana, Sandy.' But Diana is a sensitive
person who tends to turn back from nothing rather than cause trouble,
and I heard her replying—no matter what the trembling of her heart,
'No . . . I'll come . . . Sandy.' And what could I do but follow?

'Are you coming, Ernest?'

'Oh, yes, Sandy. . . . Yes, I'm coming.'

At one time in that tunnel it seemed that its floor was scraping my
breast and its roof my shoulder-blades. Far ahead, after a while, a disc
of daylight encouraged one to endure and infiltrate onward. But it
was a breathless relief to issue into that daylight and be a whole man
again, a homo erectus.

Across the same valley is 'Corvus', a climb graded, I think, as a
Severe, but this flatters it. Climbs get their classification from their
most difficult pitch—from pitches that old climbers call 'interesting'—
and there's only one severe pitch on Corvus.

This pitch, as far as I remember, is a blinded turn round a vertical
face of rock where footholds and handholds are not of the best.
Once again I was climbing last on the rope with a good old climber,
Commander Rylands, lying between me and Diana, and Sandy as usual
leading; so Diana arrived at this pitch long before I did. I heard
Sandy's voice, 'Now this is an interesting bit, Diana'; and I knew that

it was disgusting, not only from this terrible word 'interesting', but because Diana, not garrulous as a rule, would always, at any pitch of which she hated the sight, became voluble in her affirmations that she was coming, that she was quite all right, that she could do it, and that Sandy needn't worry. I knew from these rapid and voluble assertions what to expect.

But, for my part, I had no need to be afraid. I never did when Commander Rylands, R.N. lay above me on the rope, because if I was in any difficulty he just, so to say, weighed anchor (I being the anchor) and drew me aboard. On this occasion when I had a moment of difficulty on an interesting foothold, he pulled me to the required shore like a captain's gig. Once, on another day when I was lying second on the rope with the Commander below me and Diana lying last he, when he arrived at my belay, sent up a call to Sandy high above, 'There's only Mrs Mortimer to come now'; and we all wondered who Mrs Mortimer was, and how she'd become attached to the rope. It was, of course, a mistake for 'Mrs Raymond', he remembering the name of our distinguished critic on the *Sunday Times* more easily than mine. I am well used to being introduced at parties with the words 'Meet Mr Raymond Mortimer' or 'This is Mr Raymond Chandler' or 'You know Mr Raymond Gram Swing, don't you?'

Later Diana and I were to find valuable climbing friends in Maurice and Gloria Guinness, both climbers of a standard dizzily higher than ours. I have records of happy Lakeland climbs with the Guinnesses and Sandy and Tobit on Shepherd's Crag, Cam Crag, Donkey's Ears, Far South Route, Mountain Way, Knitting How, and The January Crack in Birkness Coomb. On this last I lost a toe-hold, swung on the rope like a pendulum, Maurice close behind arresting this aberration and re-establishing my true position and my dignity.

My only serious fall was a lamentably undistinguished affair. It happened on no 'interesting' pitch. We had been climbing with Tobit Birt somewhere on Rosthwaite Fell and were returning home down the grass above the lovely little village of Stonethwaite. The grassy slope here is abnormally steep, but it is crossed none the less, like all Lakeland grass-slopes, with meandering dry-stone walls. Scrambling carelessly over one of these walls I dislodged heavy lumps from the top and fell rolling down the steep slope with a lump of rock following me. Nicely rounded, it travelled on after I had slowed up, and caught me on the left side of the head—not on the summit, or I don't know what would have happened—and, having torn my face, travelled in-differently on to Stonethwaite.

The blood flowed generously, and I looked much worse than I felt. Indeed I learned then that a fall and a mighty blow on the head, if not too painful, produces an excitement that has the qualities of euphoria. My dominant thought was a pleasing one, namely that the first-aid kit which I had carried in my rucksack for years had at last justified its long sleep there. Tobit was already in Holy Orders and therefore a most suitable person to rush up and administer first-aid and spiritual comfort, which tasks he discharged expertly—not that I needed com-fort because I was possessed by this odd liveliness. When he had wiped away the blood and bandaged my head and face we went down the slope to Stonethwaite. Here a kindly farmer, Mr Connor, produced a van and motored us back to the Scafell Hotel. In the hotel a pleasant young guest immediately offered to motor me to Keswick Hospital, and while he was gone to get his car, there happened something that has always amused me. I might be lively behind my bandages and blood, but Diana was green. And the manageress, our good friend Rietta Guthrie, taking one look at her, dashed into the bar and brought out 'on the house', a double whisky for her. I, seated on a chair, got nothing. Clinically, it would have been a mistake to give me whisky or brandy, after shock, but greatly as I admire Rietta Guthrie, and good though she may be at first aid, I suspect that this was not the consideration which, at the moment, governed her movement. It was purely a matter of 'woman to woman'.

Keswick was seven miles away, and in the young man's nice little car, of which no doubt he was proud, there was a risk of my blood dripping on to it, and Diana feared all the way, in this tearing, swinging car, that she was going to be sick in it. But we got to the hospital without stain, and there they laid me on a wheeled operation trolley, put stitches all round my left eye and an elaborate bandage round my head.

And thereafter for many days I had, as on the roadway outside Railway Wood in Ypres III, a head-bandage of which a man could be proud. Proud and pleased because, as at Ypres, there was little pain behind this impressive surgical dressing; and, two days later we were climbing (I ask your pardon) 'walking' to the rocky summits of Glaramara.

The bandage was still round my head and padded over the eye

when we returned home, and I confess that I was not averse to taking it into the streets of Hampstead for friends to see. And it was a disappointment that not one person whom I met exclaimed, 'Oh, what have you been doing?' or words of like interest and sympathy. They said, 'You're back, are you?' as people do when you are standing in front of them, and 'How is Diana?' I was, of course, well pleased to be able to answer, 'She's fine, thank you'; but this was not, just then, the matter on which my mind was engaged. It seems remarkable that with a broad white bandage over an eye I never got that question, but it is the truth that I did not, and that I was disappointed. I did not until one afternoon I arrived at my club, the Garrick, and walked, bandage and all, into the corridor where we hang our coats, dispose of our brief-cases, and weigh ourselves on the scales if we're getting anxious. It is a long corridor and, as I entered it, I saw my good friend, and fine actor, the late Sir Donald Wolfit, at its further end, hanging up a coat. There were no others in the corridor. Silence possessed it and, it being mid-afternoon when the club rooms are deserted, silence stood all round it. Donald hung hat and coat, straightened his shoulders, turned, saw me, saw the bandage, took two steps towards me, and, in his grandest tragic manner, not surpassed when playing 'Lear' or 'Hamlet' breathed a long, low 'Ohhh . . .!' He might have been expressing the extreme sadness of death, and one could imagine that for the rest of the afternoon he would 'draw his breath in pain to tell my story'.

I troubled no more about the lack of interest and sympathy in the Hampstead streets. That magnificent 'Oh!', scarcely breaking the silence of an empty lobby but of a kind to be audible in a back row at Drury Lane, healed all. What could man or woman desire more?

6

PAMELA

I stated above that Pamela Frankau made a fine Hampstead councillor, after her runaway victory in the year of Orpington 'until illness in a savage form struck her down'. Rather it was a series of cruel sicknesses. While on a visit to America she was struck down by an encephalitus virus and for many weeks desperately ill and gravely suffering. She came back to England as an invalid, and I remember her lying in the London Clinic, signing for her friends copies of her newly published novel, *Sing for Your Supper*. This was the first novel of a trilogy which had all her heart at this time; it was to be called *Clothes of a King's Son*. Her recovery was slow but remarkable, the triumph of a strong, living, fighting spirit. We all know that the mind or spirit has power over the body, but during my life I have encountered cases which suggested that this power is greater—and perhaps far greater—than we know. Pamela was one of these. In time she seemed all her gay, laughing self again. But it had been a battle, and she had to fight to finish the second volume of the trilogy, *Slaves of the Lamp*. It is a long book, and the typing (by Diana) was completed only a few days before Pamela was struck down again and had to go into hospital for an operation for cancer. The outcome of the operation seemed successful, and again we had Pamela as our companion abounding with creative wit, laughter, and lively ideas for her books (and ours), though the unsparing concentration which a writer needs could still be difficult, and she had to struggle to complete the trilogy's third volume, *Over the Mountains*.

Then, greatly to my surprise and to something like indignation, for though it was my seventy-eighth year I had never once been in hospital (except an army hospital when the fault was not mine but a battlefield's) it was my turn to be hurried into hospital for an operation. I was the more surprised and indignant because, except for one painless symptom, I was feeling perfectly well and full of energy.

But into the Hampstead General Hospital I was driven.

During my five weeks there I learned some fine things about other people and some less admirable things about myself.

I suppose we all, or most of us, want to be loved and a focus of interest to others, but Heaven help us if we all feel precisely what I did when the surgeon, to my shock, on my first visit to him told me that I should have to have this operation. In my reaction to this statement there was, as well as dismay, an undeniable pride. I walked up the Hampstead High Street longing (if I'm to be frank) to get home and tell everybody the news, and to be an important centre of interest and affection. Thinking more, you perceive, of my own pleasure than of their distress. The interest and sympathy were as gratifying as any man could desire, though there were less pleasing moments, as when a compassionate woman, eager only to show her ebullient sympathy, said, 'You must take care of yourself afterwards. It often takes months to recover from an operation like that, and sometimes you're never the same again.'

And then, when I was comfortably in my hospital bed, was this basic hunger to be an object of interest and sympathy adequately ministered to? It was. The 'Get Well' cards, the flowers, the potted plants, the letters, the bottles of eau-de-Cologne, of wine, of champagne that arrived! It was certainly the only time in a long life (I was in my seventy-eighth year as I have said) that the supply of love and interest forthcoming was adequate to an outrageous appetite for it. Indeed when this flood of gifts began to abate I found myself, somewhat to my shame, thinking, not only of the wonderful friends who had sent their offerings, but of those who as yet had failed to do so. I felt disappointed in them. Even hurt.

In less self-centred moments it was, I thought, a revelation of the human animal's disgusting power to absorb the interest and love of friends, even at the price of anxiety to them. Into my mind crept the memory of a celebrated actress who said with bewildering honesty, 'I've no particular use for criticism of me. I'll settle at any time for fulsome flattery.'

Well, here was I in quite the pleasantest bed of the Victor Ward in Hampstead General Hospital, a bed in a spacious bay with three windows overlooking the garden. It was at the entrance end of the ward, so I had the whole long room before my eyes and was able to study, with no small interest, all that goes on in a surgical ward. I had, so to say, a ring-side seat. And in this ring-side seat, propped up on the back-rest with cosy pillows I gave myself to a fascinated, novelist's study, of nurses, sisters, doctors, surgeons, students, and patients. With a note-book.

And what emerges from that notebook is something far more pleasing than the sorry revelation about myself. I must insist that what follows is not romantic or sentimental but a simple statement of an objective fact. The fact is this: in a surgical ward of the right kind of hospital one sees much of the best of human nature isolated and dramatized before one's eyes.

What was dramatized for me all day, and day after day, in this hospital at least, was the goodwill of humans to humans instead of the inhumanity so rife outside all hospital walls, the patience with suffering, the instant help to anyone in pain—in a word, the neighbourliness of the Samaritan.

I am sure that young nurses are often far from perfect in places outside their wards—in the Nurses' Home perhaps, in their own homes (as parents might attest), in the company of boy-friends—but it is a truth that during my five weeks in the Victor Ward of Hampstead General I never saw one of the student nurses or staff nurses other than speedy with help or gay with comfort for any of us patients—and some could be awkward at times. I was so myself when experiencing the after-effects of the anaesthetic—'Lie down, Mr Raymond! Lie *down*!' (Though I'm afraid they said '*Lay* down'.) 'You mustn't be silly. Lay down now—' but I put up a good fight with about three of them. A continuing fight, but by close of play they had won. So, along with tribute to nurses, goes another unpleasing revelation about oneself: the anaesthetic uncovers the troublesome, unco-operative, discourteous, self-centred creature who lies buried within us all. I was ashamed of this person and tried to be co-operative, obedient and uncomplaining after this valuable introduction to him.

There is a rooted potentiality for good in human beings as well as for evil, and what I am trying to say is that it was exhilarating to see this potentiality induced in young student nurses of eighteen, nineteen, and twenty, and to watch it daily. Surely it is not commonplace but remarkable, the gentleness with which a young nurse will dress the operation wound of someone of whom she knows nothing—as if he were well worth preserving. In this connexion I had a happy experience. I was chosen to be the rabbit on the slab when one young student was to take her exam, before two alarming examiners, in the dressing of a wound. She and I passed the test with distinction; she active, I passive; within my 'tent', its curtains drawn, and the examiners watching narrowly. Nay, let me not be guilty of understatement: we passed First of All.

What I have said about the nurses appeared equally true of the patients, elderly men, most of them. Maybe when at home or at their work they could be selfish and difficult—and probably venomous at the wheels of their cars when drivers ahead of them were behaving idiotically. But here in the Victor Ward they plainly delighted to help the nurses, wheeling the chairs of some patients, taking round the tea-trolley, supporting the halt or the weak to the lavatories, visiting those in pain to offer hope and encouragement, tying the awkward tapes of our operation gowns, and always saluting the operation trolley with 'Good luck. All the best, old man.' In a sentence, enacting before me in a hospital ward the Good Neighbour, the Good Samaritan.

§

Mine was an intestinal operation and called 'serious' but it involved no such suffering as Pam's illnesses. Nevertheless, throughout my weeks in hospital, Pamela, though still in much pain which the doctor at first diagnosed as arthritic, sent me every day, by Diana's hand, brilliantly ludicrous postcards for my entertainment and encouragement. No better Samaritan than Pam, and who so amusing? I am inclined to put it that she set all her contributions to my help 'on her own donkey'—a brilliant beast. All these cards were addressed to 'Chairman Ernie' because on her birthday, a few weeks before, honouring a now established custom between us, I had composed a poem for the festival and, being thoroughly bored just then by daily mention in the newspapers of 'Chairman Mao's Thought', and of the 'Cultural Revolution' in China with Red Guards brandishing copies of 'Chairman Mao's Thought', I had inscribed my poem as 'From Chairman Ernie's Thought'.

I must further explain that our local newspaper is the *Hampstead and Highgate Express*, affectionately known to every citizen in these two towns as the *Ham and High*. Between the heights of Hampstead and Highgate lies our rolling Heath and accordingly a main feature of the *Ham and High* is a gossip page signed by 'Heathman'. Often its 'pithy paragraphs' cover the deeds of councillors, so Pamela created for my diversion in hospital, a journalist of similar proclivities, by name 'Heathwoman'.

All these postcards were punctiliously numbered, and first is a violently coloured picture of a gigantic beefeater, the Yeoman Gaoler of the Tower of London, in his full Tudor uniform, holding a murderous halberd or execution axe. Pamela's inscription is 'A striking picture of Lady Brooke of Ystradfellte'—our celebrated and popular Barbara Brooke—'in the costume which won her First Prize at the Conservative's Fancy Dress Ball last Monday. "I made it myself," Lady Brooke told Heathwoman.'

No. 2 is a coloured postcard of Piccadilly Circus with Eros in its centre; and the inscription: 'Opening! The new circular shopping piazza built above Hampstead's former Whitestone Pond. On concrete, at centre, a statue [Eros] of a former Mayor of Hampstead, Councillor Luigi Denza.' No. 3 is our famous Spaniard's Inn; the inscription: 'The Gracious Home of Miss Pamela Frankau (former councillor and novelist) caught at closing time. Asterisk masks the window of—' but never mind where. No. 4 is a picture of the Drum Major, Grenadier Guards with insets of the Irish Guards band, the Trooping the Colour, and the Yeoman Warders of the Tower. Inscription: 'Bravo, Geoffrey —' Councillor Geoffrey Finsberg is our Parliamentary Conservative candidate—'Wednesday was a great day for Hampstead's Tory Leader. He obtained commissions in the Horse, Irish, and Grenadier Guards simultaneously, and was elected Yeoman Warder of the Tower. "It came as a complete surprise," said Mr Finsberg.'

No. 5 shows Romney's House in Hampstead with a dormobile passing it on the left, and a woman with a parcel hurrying up the hill on the right. Inscription: 'Councillor Miss A.B.C.'—my substitutions —'on her mercy dash in dormobile, seen left, with family-planning pills for Hampstead Girl Guides. Councillor Miss X.Y.Z. follows on foot with reinforcements. "We remember how it felt," said the ladies in nostalgic interview with Heathwoman.'

No. 6 is our famous Old Bull and Bush with the figure of an attractive girl on horseback riding by. The figure of the girl is far from clear, and Pamela's inscription is: 'The Reverend P . . . Q . . . [name of a local clergyman] makes his dramatic horseback protest against Hampstead alcoholism. Heathwoman snapped him passing one of the 250 public houses at whose doors he scattered temperance leaflets. "I could do with a drink," said the cleric humorously.'

And so they went on, these daily doses of comfort and joy from Pamela. Some were stuck down in envelopes addressed 'Chairman Ernie, Private and Confidential', as well they might be. Many gave great amusement to the nurses, but a few of them I judged unsuitable for display by an elderly patient to young student nurses (not that I supposed there was much on this earth they didn't know all about). Such a one was a poem of which I will give you only the opening lines. In the first days after my operation I was tethered to my bed by three leashes, a saline 'drip', a local anaesthetic 'drip', and inevitably a catheter. Pamela's poem was to comfort me about this last.

Pamela was a devout Roman Catholic, and sometimes even, I would think, too warm in her intolerance of, and her antagonism to, the irreligious, but like many other of the devoutest Catholics, and unlike more puritan souls, she delighted in impish irreverence, and enjoyed her reasonable ration of bawdry. It is only I who have substituted dots for letters in certain words.

A PRAYER TO A LITTLE KNOWN SAINT

Blessed St Catheter, pray for us, please.
We're all of us nuns, but none of us p . . .
The Mother Superior gave us a mixture
But it ain't done a thing for our communal stricture.
We've been round our rosaries telling each bead;
By this time we certainly ought to—

but the rest I think I had better keep to myself. Saving only her descriptive note at the end: 'Written in the London Clinic by an unsuccessful novelist, P. Frankau, while awaiting the catheter. You have my deepest sympathy, Comrade Chairman, and *much* love.'

Then a letter headed:

Hampstead and Highgate Express

'Dear Mr Raymond,

We write on behalf of our employee, 'Heathwoman' who wants, we understand, to send you a proof of her diary for this week's review. We are delighted to know of your interest in her work, but we are sure you will understand that, owing to libel cases pending from

A) Lady Brooke
B) Councillor Luigi Denza
C) Mr Geoffrey Finsberg
D) Councillor Miss A.B.C.
E) Councillor Miss X.Y.Z.
F) Miss Pamela Frankau

Heathwoman is at present busy with her legal advisers. In the unlikely event of her obtaining future employment with us (the total damages claimed amounting to £200,000) she will be communicating with you shortly.

'May we offer you apologies for inconvenience caused and our sincere good wishes for your complete recovery.

Yours devotedly,

THE EDITOR

'N.B. Dictated by Editor who suffered a stroke before signing it. Secretary.'

§

Throughout these years of intermittent pain and increasing illness Pamela's main task was to complete, whatever the struggle, her fine trilogy, *Clothes of a King's Son*. But she was also beset through these years by an inspiration for a 'suspense' or 'mystery' novel. She had never written such a book before; now, with *Over the Mountains* finished, and the trilogy in being, this new and exciting idea took full possession of her. She gave herself to it, come pain, come weariness, come exhaustion, with laborious efforts at concentration that suggested a fear that she might not be given the time to complete it. Either in her house or in our flat she would discuss it with my wife and Margaret Webster, these two being part of the very small company who had been told, under orders of secrecy, what the surprise ending was to be. The title, she was resolved, was to be *Colonel Blessington*; and those who have read it will have seen how terse and right was this simple title. By early '67, when she was writing the comic postcards and letters for my diversion in hospital, she had accumulated a pile of manuscript books, books of notes, and even, as new ideas, or changes in the book's structure occurred to her, a tape-recording so that these later ideas might be preserved. At the end of March, just before I left hospital (where, unlike her, I had suffered little pain) Dr Raymond Greene came to her home and told her that an X-ray showed her pains to be caused by cancer in the bone. It was then that she asked Diana to come and help her finish the book. They worked together but . . . the end came too soon. A few weeks were all that were left to her. She died in the first days of June. Within only weeks of her gay, ribald, daily comforting of me in hospital, Pamela was dead.

Her letter written on the eve of my operation, accompanying two mascots—two pendent, long-eared, jewel-eyed golden rabbits—had been as follows:

'My darling,

I have been trying to figure what really useful present I can send you. Being, as you know, well trained in hospital needs, my experienced research has come up with these two rabbits.

'They have the following advantages:

(a) They need no feeding, watering or attention.
(b) They can, if not required by your bedside, entertain Carruthers at home until your return—'

Carruthers is an idiot but charming woollen dog on our bedroom mantelpiece at home—

'(c) They are powerful luck-bringers, having once belonged to an old magician named John D. Rockefeller.
(d) Both are members of the Garrick Club and espouse the decent principles of the Liberal Party as it was in its best days.
(e) They have read ALL your books and have been heard to murmur, "He's the greatest, he's the most" when ordering them at the Times Bookshop.
(f) They are guaranteed not to produce litters of less acceptable rabbits.

'So there you are. Best of luck, darling, and huge prayers.

Pamela.'

§

At the request of Pamela's sister, Ursula d'Arch-Smith, and of Peggy Webster Diana undertook willingly, ardently, to edit, order, and add the known end to *Colonel Blessington*. I think it is fair to say that no one else in the world could have done this, unless it was Margaret Webster herself, for only they knew everything that Pamela had in mind; but Margaret, who had to go on a lecture tour and play-producing visit to America, handed over to Diana all the manuscript books, the books of notes, and the tape recording. Diana, too, had the

advantage of being herself a skilled novelist, having published a
dozen novels of her own, two of which were Book Society choices.
It involved long and heavy labours, so massed were the notes and
so complex the later ideas for the shaping of the story; as Peggy
Webster has said, 'Only God, Ernest and I know what the labours
were.' But these were labours of love. When the task was finished
there was joy for all in the belief that a book on which Pamela's
heart had been set now existed in the form and shape she wished it to
possess.

I was asked by the Royal Society of Literature to write the obituary
tribute to Pamela in their Annual Report, and they allow me to quote
from it here.

'I can offer no greater tribute to the quality of Pamela Frankau as
a human being than to say that when word came that she was dead,
my immediate feeling was a sudden, unforeseen heightening of my
belief in (or if belief is too strong a word, my hope of) human immortality. In what this immortality will consist I cannot even guess: for
me the word just connotes that—perhaps, or probably—the human
spirit is indestructible. I do not think that this sudden surge of faith,
when I heard of Pamela's death, was a mere "wish-fulfilment" thought.
Such an easy motion of the heart would have been unworthy of
Pamela. It was just that I felt it intellectually almost impossible to
believe that the splendid intelligence, the keen and eager vision, and
the large, loving, laughing heart which were Pamela could cease to be.
To believe that anything so brilliant, so shining with a glow that
surely came from the very stuff of Reality, could have suddenly become
nothing seemed analogous, in a small way, to supposing that the sun
is not still there because night has intervened. And this access of faith
was increased as I recalled her mental superiority to grave ill-health
and ever-increasing weakness. The last words of her will, written
when she believed that death was near, are "I give praise and thanks
to Almighty God for the gift of life. I thank my loves, my friends, my
acquaintances, and my benefactors for helping to make it such a good
adventure."

'This superiority was not just courage in pain; it was exactly what
the word says: superiority to it. She was somehow above it. Well
above it, and so much so that we, her friends, would all too often
completely forget it in the gaiety and excitement of her presence. To

remember this radiant superiority is to live with the hope that it is now independent of the greatest weakness of all which is death.'

§

I would like to quote also from my wife's tribute, because it was accepted by many as carrying the right words for Pamela. It was written by special request of our *Hampstead and Highgate Express* which had known Pamela so well and enjoyed her as local councillor, writer, and celebrity.

'Brilliant wit and profound compassion are not most commonly harnessed together: in Pamela they were fused to make a person who was unique. She was unrepeatable: her loss cuts deep.

'Her wit was continual, entirely her own, surviving extremes of adversity and pain. Yet it was not only wit—it had at the heart a wisdom which threw a sudden healing light upon the world of our wraths and sorrows. She had the rare quality of being able, simply by her presence, to make you feel gayer, stronger, more able to cope with the difficulty on hand. Without her, life has lost much of its shine and colour. Our triumphs—if they come—seem less because we cannot bring them to show her; the comic absurdities of accident or word that enliven the day's ordinary round aren't quite so funny because we cannot hear her welcoming shout of laughter at our telling of them. Unlike many other brilliant talkers, she was a devoted listener. . . .

'She was received into the Roman Catholic Church in 1942, and her faith, like her courage, was a "catching" thing: in Pamela the love of God was part of fun, part of companionship, part of life: it sparked in the air around her. Only blasphemy and cruelty could shock her; she brought to the common frailties of mankind a wise tolerance laced —as always—with fun.

'She had an unfailing eye for pomposity, hypocrisy or extreme self-pity; at the first suggestion of these that one familiar eyebrow would go up: a warning that some puncturing wit would follow. Like many rapid-thinking people, she found it hard to suffer fools gladly. Yet so fundamentally loving was her nature that any momentary loss of temper was quickly regretted, quickly redressed. She was always ready to do the difficult kindnesses; the ones that take time, trouble and often courage to perform. . . .

'It was to her I brought my first adolescent writing, and she was unfailing in help and encouragement. (Unfailing too in the authentic Frankau touch: I had written some youthful overblown phrase; Pamela scribbled in the margin "Meanwhile, in a nearby mill . . .".) She always seemed to me the one who went ahead, who knew the dangers and the deeper sorrows, and gave kindly warning of them. Now she has gone ahead again.

'And in going, she has left us some of her courage; because of her we are a little stronger, more able to endure her loss.'

7

A LAST MEDITATION

I closed the first part of this volume with a meditation on the Novelist's art, and made the submission that the by-product of great novels—in other words, the unstated but implicit vision driving their author and 'falling out' from his book—must nearly always be Applied Christianity.

Two cold words I called these: a warm story which encloses their essence without speaking it, is the Good Samaritan. It is noteworthy that it was only when Christ had told his story that he became explicit and asked what was its unspoken by-product; what its fall-out. And what is it? It is just this: no vengeance; no sour retaliation by the Samaritan for the contemptuous attitude of the Jews towards his people; no racial hatred; only help by the wayside for a wounded man; everything else, his race, his religion, his hostility, his sins, all of no account, since all that mattered was his pain.

I want to close this second part, and the whole *Story of My Days*, with a statement of such faith as I have been able to achieve in this sceptical age, and a meditation—not on 'applied Christianity' which cries itself aloud in me, and suffers never a moment of scepticism—but on 'dogmatic Christianity' which proclaims the divine sanctions behind it.

In my first volume I told briefly how I relinquished Holy Orders because I could no longer say 'Firmly I believe and truly' the dogmas I had to teach to children and proclaim from the pulpit; and, still more briefly, how after forty-odd years in a desert of agnostic doubt, I found myself able to return to the Church, not again as a preaching and teaching priest but as a learning layman.

What, then, enabled me to make this return, and what have I learned, or recovered, occupying the humbler place of a layman's pew? Belief in God, however unknown, was always there. As I submitted in the first volume: all the world is mystery, and all 'being' is miracle past understanding. Take only the miracle of birth. I do not know how one can see a new-born foal, or an exquisite litter of lion cubs, or a human child brought forth into Time and our world, a little creature of vast spiritual potentials and powers, without bending in humility before the Unknown. To bend over a cradle and consider face, features and hands of a baby say a month old, is for me to be in the presence of something that has left rationality and intellectuality and common sense lagging far behind. These merely human reasonings can look at this creation only from their distance far behind, and with a defeated wonder. I can see where a reverent agnostic stands in the presence of such a miracle, but I can find no footing for the dogmatic atheist anywhere. Or for the 'Logical' Humanist.

All life is magical, not logical.

Thus I could always say happily the first of the three paragraphs in the great Creeds of the Church. But what of the second paragraph with its Christological dogmas? This kept me in my wilderness for many years. Indeed till only a few years ago. Then in the spring of 1966 I went back to the Holy Land, not 'in the steps of St Francis', but very much in the steps of his sole inspirer and master, wondering if I could recover in these haunted places something of the faith which had made Francis what he was. And of all the places that had known his young master's sandalled feet—Capernaum, Galilee-side, the Temple area, Bethany—most came to me from the old trackway over the hill of Olivet—the short cut from Bethany to Jerusalem—which, beyond question Christ must have trodden when leaving Bethany behind him on the other side of the hill and coming towards Jerusalem across the Kidron valley. I tried to set down my experiences on that rough white track in a novel whose central character is wholly fictitious, but, inevitably his experiences on the Bethany track are mine. It is difficult to retell them now in words other than those which I chose then with care, and which persist in denying me any satisfaction when I try to change them. So I surrender to this implacable resistance, and will quote with only small verbal changes two passages from that story.

The first:

'I had a poignant reason for coming this way. It must have been down this rough, white, sun-bleached track, the short way over the hill, that Christ came with his disciples when, for the last time he left his usual haven of rest, a family home in Bethany, and set his face towards Jerusalem that he might meet his hour.

'Standing there, with Bethany behind me, under the hill, and that stony white road before me, I prepared my mind like an empty stage for such thoughts as would come. And the first thought to occupy and fill the stage was one that for me, alike in my days of faith and of doubt, has always belonged to this age-old stretch of wheel-beaten track dropping down from Olivet's ridge to the Kidron Valley; one that has never failed to charge itself with its own tremendous question.

'Probably the sun was low over Jerusalem, or almost setting behind it, when Christ said good-bye—and with what sadness—to the three dear friends at Bethany and came slowly over the hill to pass where I was standing now. . . .

'I stood there waiting for the sun to fall lower and then, like that little company of thirteen men, walked down to where, by the Paternoster Church, the whole city of Jerusalem, walls and gates, towers and domes, broke upon my view. When they saw it, that Passover eve, it must have been gaily adorned for the feast, with the tents of the crowding pilgrims everywhere around its walls—down among the cypresses and tombs in the valley, and over the slopes of the hills that "stand about Jerusalem".

'Always as I picture this moment when, coming down the slope, Christ saw the city thus arrayed I see him walking a pace or two ahead of the others because I remember Mark's words, so vivid, so pregnant, of another approach to Jerusalem, "Jesus went before them; and they were amazed; and as they followed, they were afraid." One can almost hear the hush, as they looked towards him, and, in silence, walked behind.

'These words of bewildered fear and love went with me as I too walked down the road with Jerusalem before me, following, as it were, behind that little company of long ago, and feeling with them much of their bewilderment, some of their nameless fear, and certainly some of their love. Who *was* he? *What* was he, this strange, strong, rather stormy, dedicated, loving young man, Jeshua ben Joseph, a country boy, as is so plain from all his stories about shepherds, birds, flowers, seeds and harvest?

'Who? I walked on with this one-thousand-nine-hundred-year question.

'How could I believe, try as I would, try as I longed to, that yonder young man, leading his little company, had hung the stars in place, set the evolutionary ages rolling, and was God Incarnate walking down the Bethany track with friends; God Incarnate coming for his break into history?'

And the other (my central character is now kneeling in a London church. The service is a Solemn Eucharist with full ceremonial, and he is watching the people other than himself going up to the altar rails to take communion):

'The memory which came to the surface and sent my thoughts in a new direction as I knelt there was that of my lonely walk down the slope of Olivet, trying to picture Christ coming down it for the last time—to accept the dreadful cup which he knew stood before him. I was thinking, How could one do other than love this young man coming with his disciples down that track, when the one thing about him of which we could feel certain was that he was coming determined to show the world what Love—and the God who is Love—really were. "I, if I be lifted up, will draw all men unto me." . . . How other than love him and in some way range oneself with him, as all these people, young and old, simple and unlearned, or wise and scholarly, were doing?

'The hymn ended, the last few communicants trickled past me to their pews, the organist was playing gently his variations on the hymn's melody till the priest should be ready to say the Paternoster, and it was in these quiet moments that I came to a decision.

'Belief in an unknown God had never been any difficulty to me. As surely as materialist and humanist believed in a rational order of the universe which could never be fully known but would not fail them, so surely I believed in a God who could never be known. Each of these axioms, after all, was but a transcendental faith and looked rather like the same thing, some of us calling it Nature's Laws and some of us calling it God. But on this Sunday in this old church, there was nothing easy about a full, orthodox faith in that young man on the Bethany track whom I could but love, and, in a sense, worship; and my decision was this, as we waited on our knees, silently, for his own Paternoster. "Surely," I decided, "the one thing to do is to give oneself to a love one feels, and leave all else with the God unknown."

'Next time then—or perhaps one day—I would go up with the people and share with them in their communion. I would go in a kind of blind love and trust, asking pardon—or understanding—for a faith so unsure. And as I thought this there leapt into my mind three magnificent words of Aristotle's—Aristotle whom no one yet, in two millenia, has charged with sentimentality, Aristotle, the earthbound philosopher whose feet were ever on the ground rather than among the stars. His God whom, as an austere philosopher he must hold to be impassive, immutable, and immobile was none the less able, though in stillness and rest, to move all things; and his words for this were: κινεῖ ὡς ἐρώμενον: "he moves us—" or, if you like—"he draws us as a beloved".

'These words could be exactly the truth for me about that young man on the Bethany roadway; *and* for the splendid ceremonial in this Solemn Eucharist. It drew me as a beloved. I remembered Clem saying that perhaps he ought to have been a Quaker because their silences would suit him so much better than my High Church goings-on. Well, perhaps I was a Quaker too, but in this different sense: that Quakers demanded no certainties from their followers. But if I was such a Quaker I was also one who, untypically, loved and needed services like these: majestic parables of God's love given to men, and their love returned to him with every beauty they could offer. An Anglo-Catholic Quaker, let us say. Believing much, if less than all. While hoping all.'

§

In that church on that Sunday (I am speaking now in my own person) I remembered how many devoted priests had allowed to me that there must always be this halo of doubt—or, perhaps, 'a sacred halo of wondering' would be a safer phrase—around both the Triune nature of God and the Deity of Jesus, because, just as our limited human minds cannot enfold and comprehend a Triunity in God, so in the Deity of Jesus, they cannot encompass a narrowing down of the Absolute into the limited and relative; of the Infinite into the finite; and a dwindling down of an Existence in the Eternal Stillness into an existence obeying the conditions of time and space. One cannot escape this aura of difficult wonder, and to escape it—to be freed from it—would turn one's faith into the facile acceptance of children or slaves, believing without thought or passion whatever Authority bids them believe.

And while I was thinking this, there came the thought that if, admitting the inescapable question that surrounded the nature of Christ, I could still say, 'I accept the mystery and let my trust and hope rest in it,' then there seemed to follow a very strange, equally mysterious, but inspiring fact: this, that the God whom one must accept as the ground and spring of our being (who else can be?) was not just a lonely and monotonous Unity but a Being in whom there was already—before we were born, before the world was created—a habit of reciprocal love—

since the mystery of More-than-one-Person in God is an indispensable corollary from the Deity of Christ; and that thus the source of our being, or if you prefer it, 'the God within us' is already a habit of reciprocal love. And I seemed to see then how much richer was the doctrine of a Triune God (however incomprehensible) than the easier one of a single and lonely God as worshipped by Unitarians, and called by Matthew Arnold no more than 'the enduring power, not ourselves, which makes for righteousness' or by Whitehead 'that which is behind, beyond, and within the eternal flux of things'. The cold and the poverty of naked Theism!

Well, there it is. All is but a gazing into the ineffable. Perhaps Goethe's words are as good as any, when he makes his Faust say to Gretchen what one can only believe was Goethe's own belief:

> Feel'st not
> Throbbing through head and heart the force
> Still weaving its eternal secret
> Visible, invisible, about thy life?
> Vast as it is, fill with that force thy heart,
> And when thou in the feeling wholly blessed art,
> Call it then what thou wilt—call it Love, God, Life.
> I have no name to give it. Feeling is all in all.
> The name is sound and smoke,
> Obscuring Heaven's clear glow.

§

Among those who received *The Story of My Days* so kindly there were some who complained that the record of my recovery of faith and my return to the Church was treated too briefly. This was a just criticism, so I set out to meet it in the six or seven foregoing pages.

But even so, even then, the dedicatees of my first volume (my children, and my grandson) insisted that it could be the most important subject of all if it were made, not so much a section of autobiography as a closing attempt at a Statement of Faith for men to live by in these desperate years when so much of sanity, morality, and humanity seems to be falling into ruin, and Mankind, in many ways to be converting itself into a caricature of what it ought to be.

My elder son, the Wing-Commander, who, as I have told, inspired this second volume (and must bear some responsibility for it) now suggested, not unimperiously, that a third book—on the Possibility of Faith—ought to be written, both from the viewpoint of a long life and my eightieth year; and that this third volume might well come out of the heart of the one subject on which I can claim some scholarship, the story of St Francis of Assisi, and the history of Franciscanism.

Thirty-one years ago I published my *In the Steps of St Francis*, and in the closing words of its introduction wrote that its purpose was 'to make as vivid and memorable as possible the impact of Francis upon this modern age of ours which, if I mistake not, is more sadly disillusioned than any period within the last seven centuries and more sick for a God and a sanctity'.

That was written in 1937 and published in 1938 on the day of the Munich Agreement; and if those words had some truth then, surely they are totally true now—except perhaps for the over-strong word 'sanctity'. What have the thirty subsequent years not seen? Genocide. . . . Torture. . . . Hiroshima. . . . The world-destructive forces, lying in the dust of the earth, unhoused and unloosed, and ready.

So I took some fire at the idea of a final volume which should be a Statement of the everlasting, ever undated, ever modern, ever absolute (not relative) challenge to the world of the Little Poor Man of Assisi. It would be written in those parts of Italy where the spirit of St Francis is always present and potent. In the Vale of Rieti there hangs high on a spur of one of its encircling mountains the little white village of Poggio Bustone. So high is it that, when the mountain behind is absorbed into the night sky, the lights of Poggio Bustone look like stars. A road climbs to it in an unending spiral; and up this winding road, in the year 1209, went Francis in his brown habit and white cord. As he passed through the walls into the village, the people, whose reputation at the time was dark indeed, came running out to learn what this portent might be. And with a smile he gave them the greeting, 'Good morning, good people.'

They have never forgotten that salute. Today near the centre of the village you can see a white stone in a wall and read:

BUON GIORNO, BUONA GENTE
Saluto rivolto da San Francesco
Entrando a Poggio Bustone
nel 1209

And if you are in Poggio Bustone on 4th October, which is observed throughout the world as the anniversary of his death (though he died the evening before), and if you are in the street early enough, you will see a man with a tambourine going from house to house and knocking at each door, and calling to the people within, 'Buon giorno, buona gente.'

'Good morning, good people.' Had my first St Francis book not been one of a series with its title prescribed 'In the Steps of . . .' I should certainly have called it by these words. Together with '*Il Signore vi dia pace*' and '*Pax et bonum*', they were a favourite greeting of St Francis to all men everywhere whether good or bad, whether saints in the churches, or bandits in the woods, or faithless in the streets, or pagans in the camp of the Saracens; and they always seem to me to contain the whole meaning and message of Francis, his love for all, his labour for all, and his hope for all.

So there will come this third, and *most* emphatically, last volume of autobiography, a Full Statement of Faith Arrived At, in spite of all; and even if we are mostly sinners—and never mind to what extent we are sinning—its title shall be *Good Morning, Good People.*

INDEX